Adding *Math,* Subtracting *Tension*

Adding
Math,
Subtracting
Tension

• • • • • • • • •

A Guide to
Raising Children Who
Can Do Math

VOLUME 1
INFANCY THROUGH SECOND GRADE

Frances Stern

Illustrations by Paul O. Wilson

Talk
About
Math

©2010 Frances Stern
Illustrations ©2010 Paul O. Wilson

Book design: ℓDESKTOP.
Cover design: Rachel Perkins
Diagrams and additional illustration: Frances Stern, Adrian & Elizabeth Kitzinger

Library of Congress Control Number: 2010921401
ISBN 978-0-9843318-0-2

Published by :      Talk About Math
400 East 85th Street #4D
New York, NY 10028
info@talkaboutmath.org
www.talkaboutmath.org

Credit Page 19: FIVE LITTLE FROGS A/K/A FIVE LITTLE SPECKLED FROGS
                Traditional, Arranged by VIRGINIA PAVELKO
                ©1954 BOWMAR RECORDS
                Copyright Renewed and Assigned to BELWIN-MILLS PUBLISHING CORP.
                All Rights Controlled and Administered by ALFRED PUBLISHING CO., INC.
                All Rights Reserved

Contents

A Letter to Readers

Dear Parents, Teachers, and Caregivers,

● ● ● ● ● *How can I help my child learn math without the anxiety that so often accompanies this subject?* Parents of all backgrounds—those whose knowledge of math is small and those who use it daily in their work—share this concern. *What if I never liked math or didn't do well in it myself?* This book is intended to help you develop a positive relationship with your child by offering useful approaches to this subject and including activities that make math a source of fun. Many family pastimes can include math in a natural way while they build your child's foundation in math. By starting in your child's infancy with topics you know well, and becoming comfortable with including math in your conversations, you can develop a bond with your child that will allow you to continue to explore mathematical ideas and support your child's learning throughout the grade-school years.

Children are constantly trying to make sense of the world around them. They make observations, generalize, and ask questions. They use their natural abilities and intelligence to develop methods of solving problems of many kinds, including math. When they are asked to learn a subject without understanding it, they easily become overwhelmed and frustrated. Unfortunately, math is often taught in a manner that does not make sense to them, and they soon feel helpless and stupid. They do not realize that it is the manner of teaching and not the subject itself that is the problem.

Children's educational success and future careers depend in large part on their ability to do well on standardized tests that include math. Many parents feel inadequate in their own knowledge of math. Even those who do know the math find that the pressure of tests causes tension. Parents hope their children will have a better experience than they did, but don't know how to assist them.

Learning math involves learning its three components: **conventions, concepts**, and **skills. Conventions** are the generally agreed-upon aspects of math that must be memorized. These include the symbols we use to represent the numbers (0,1, 2, 3, . . .) and those for arithmetic operations (+, −, ×, ÷). Many people find concepts and skills difficult to separate. An example is the **concept** of addition—knowing that adding means putting two groups together and finding out how many are in the joined group. A young child may grasp this concept. When asked to add four and three, a five-year-old might count out four objects, count out three, then put the objects together and count starting from one again in order to find the total. Although this child understands well the **concept** of addition, it will be several years before she or he develops the **skills** needed to add 378 and 835: memorization of basic number facts and a practical and reliable method of adding large numbers. When lessons focus only on skills without addressing the concepts involved, many children feel lost and lose interest. When children understand what they are doing and why, they feel successful, even powerful, and are eager to do more math.

● ● ● ● ● **So what can you do?** This book will show you how to give your child a basic understanding of math, the foundation necessary to do well in this important subject and even enjoy it. The book is designed so that it does not have to be read in order. If your child already knows how to count, you might want to jump to a later chapter.

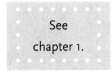

☞ Whenever a term is used that was defined in an earlier chapter, the reference is given in a sidebar.

☞ Sidebars with this icon will also indicate those activities that are illustrated by videos at ***www. talkaboutmath.org***

Sidebars with this symbol ✂ accompany illustrations with a version in the back of the book suitable for copying or cutting out for making materials to use with your children.

As you try the activities, there are some important things to keep in mind:

- Be your child's champion, not tester. Avoid putting her or him on the spot, but do notice what errors are made and work on them.

- If you forget to do math for a while, don't overdo it when you remember.

- Knowing a lot of math is not necessary—you can learn with your child.

- Watching and listening are more important than explaining or telling what to do.

If you are having fun and don't get upset by mistakes, your child will be happy to participate. All children are eager for parents' time and attention, so give it . . . with math.

—Frances Stern

Adding *Math,* Subtracting *Tension*

1

Getting Started

Counting

When a baby is born, we count her fingers and toes and measure her weight and length. Within moments of birth, numbers are a vital part of a child's life. As she grows she will need to understand and use numbers in an endless variety of ways. Her natural curiosity, her desire to do what big people do, and her innate sense of numbers will lead her to recite numbers long before she knows what they mean. Children are fascinated by numbers. As a parent, you are in a position to foster that interest, even if your knowledge of mathematics is minimal. This is because math is everywhere, and numbers are familiar to everyone. A child's math life begins with the magic words *one, two, three* . . . At first these words make little sense to her. Only gradually, with many repetitions, will they take

Just arrived on the Stork Express

To the _____ family

Name _____

Date/time _____

Weight/length _____

From the moment of birth, numbers are important in a child's life.

on meaning. By counting with your child, from infancy onwards, you can give her a healthy start to her math life. Counting is the introduction to numbers and to the whole field of mathematics.

As you enter into your life of math with your child, it will be both easier and more challenging than you expect. This is even true of counting. We learn to count at such a young age that most adults forget just how much work was required to learn it. In order to count, we must:

- memorize words

- say them in a certain order

- connect each number-word to an object to be counted (this is called "one-to-one" counting)

- recognize the increasing pattern of the numbers

- understand that the final number that we say represents the total quantity in the group

- see that the order in which we count the objects does not affect the total

- understand that the number of objects in a group remains the same, no matter how the objects are placed (this is called "conservation of number")

This is an impressive list and does not even include the need to recognize written numbers.

This chapter offers ways that you can help your child learn to count, and it includes activities that will help you create a positive mathematical relationship with your child.

MEMORIZING NUMBER WORDS AND SAYING THEM IN THE RIGHT ORDER

Throughout the world, people play counting games with babies:

One, two, three, four, five,
Once I caught a fish alive.
Six, seven, eight, nine, ten,
Then I let it go again.

They usually touch a finger as they say each number. This universal action reinforces the child's learning by combining sound and touch. It is not a coincidence that the word "digit" refers to both fingers and numbers in many languages. These games can be the beginning of playing with math with your child. You can make up your own family versions such as this one:

One little, two little, three little toesies,
Four little, five little, six little toesies,
Seven little, eight little, nine little toesies,
Ten toesies in the bath tub!

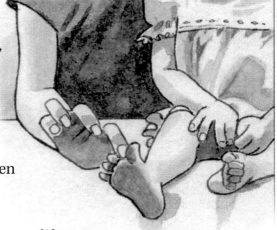

. . . *two little,* . . .

Even though your infant or toddler cannot yet understand the meaning of numbers, she is beginning to make sense of her world and make connections between things she hears, sees, and feels.

Numbers are abstract things. It may be more difficult to memorize the names for the numbers than for objects that babies can see and touch, like "book," "blanket," or "spoon." The numbers must be said in a particular order. While the same is true of nursery rhymes like "Hickory Dickory Dock," the numbers have less rhythm and no rhyme. Learning the words for numbers and their order requires many repetitions over a long time. It is helpful to realize that the names of the numbers do not settle down to a fixed pattern until the number 20. The numbers from one through twelve each have their own names. As readers, we recognize the relationship between "two," "twelve," and "twenty," but a child is not aware of this pattern. Thirteen through nineteen form a pattern, but we write thirteen by first drawing a "1" and then a "3." We say the "three" first when we say "thir-teen" and use "teen" to mean "ten." For the numbers 20 through 99, however, we say the numbers in the order in which they are written: we write "2," then "1," and say "twenty-one." You see how complicated it is—but we all learned it and your child will too.

> It is difficult for young children to learn which written number is "thirteen" and which is "thirty-one."
>
> **13**
> **31**

THINGS YOU CAN DO TO HELP YOUR CHILD LEARN TO COUNT

- Count aloud both with and without objects.
- Count little fingers and toes often, touching one as you say a number.
- Read counting books together.

Sing and chant many number songs and rhymes. See how many you can remember, learn from friends and family. The public library also has songbooks; many are in picture book format. Rhymes are especially useful when a child needs to be entertained in a confined space, such as a car, bus, or waiting in line.

HOW HIGH SHOULD YOU COUNT WITH YOUR CHILD?

● ● ● ● ● **That depends on the context.** Any time you are counting actual objects for a purpose, you will count as high as you need. At those times, make sure to count aloud so that your child both hears and sees you. In this way the child learns that math is useful.

SAYING NUMBERS IS DIFFERENT FROM KNOWING THEIR MEANING

● ● ● ● ● **A two-year-old can learn** to say *one two three four five*. This skill is different from being able to count objects. Most two-year-olds can count only two objects. **Always remember—each child is different.** At three years of age, the number three usually has meaning, but a three-year-old is likely to be able to *say* the numbers to ten if she has heard them since infancy.

There is a wide range of skills among kindergartners depending on their experience. While teachers have many students to teach, you, as a parent, are in a position to provide appropriate experiences, geared precisely to what your child already knows and needs to learn. If your child does not yet know how to count, begin to count things with her. If she can count to ten, begin working on the names of the numbers above ten. See how many objects she can count accurately and, very gradually, increase the number of items you give her to count, adding only one more to the amount she counts accurately.

WHAT SHOULD YOU COUNT WITH YOUR CHILD?

Everything you can think of! Banana slices as you prepare a snack, sections of an orange, the number of eggs to be used for breakfast. Counting food has the extra advantage of contributing the senses of taste and smell to the counting experience. Count silverware and dishes as you set the table, the number of people in the family, legs on a dog, pennies in a penny collection, blocks you can stack in a tower, toys your child wants to put into a pile, trees in your yard, people in line, groceries in your cart, cars.

Sometimes you will count only a few items, other times the count may be quite high. Be on the lookout for things to count and let your child choose things for you to count together—maybe silly things like hiccups. This way it becomes her game, not only yours. You can laugh and do math together!

Counting can actually ease tension instead of causing it. One day, on a family hike, my husband was walking ahead with our older daughter while I was in the rear with a tired, cranky youngster refusing to continue. We needed to climb

You can count items together as you place them in the cart.

a long stairway to the top of an overlook where we would picnic and rest—and the ones on top had the food. I offered that she choose the number of steps we would climb before resting. Expecting something in the neighborhood of *5*, I was delighted when she said *30*. With both us counting the steps, in a short time we reached the top, in a good mood, aided by the fact that her guess of the total number of steps was better than mine.

RECOGNIZING THE PATTERN OF THE NUMBERS AND COUNTING PAST TWENTY

● ● ● ● ● **Children must recognize the "one" to "nine" pattern** that follows twenty ("twenty-**one,**" "twenty-**two,**" "twenty-**three**" . . .). This pattern is usually learned long before counting by tens is memorized in order. This is an important part of learning to count. This means that a child may sometimes remember to say *forty* after *thirty-nine* and sometimes forget and insert *twenty* or *ninety*. **Don't worry about these errors.** This is a complex process, but with practice, all children master it. To help your child, count out loud together.

Taking turns saying the numbers is a friendly way to practice counting.

You can watch a video of this activity. Choose the button "Help your child to count even better."

www.talkaboutmath.org

Practice taking turns saying the numbers. Let your child say *one,* you say *two,* your child says *three,* and so on. If your child begins the count, you will be the one to say the difficult-to-remember numbers: *twenty, thirty, forty* . . . To help your child memorize those words, you can also practice chanting by tens up to 100.

THE FINAL NUMBER SAID IS THE TOTAL IN THE GROUP

An aspect of counting that we take for granted is that the last number said tells us the total amount in the group, not something about the last object counted. This is quite an abstract idea that will develop over time after a child has a great amount of experience participating in useful counting.

The repetition of numbers seems to have an amazing power over young children—they love to count. I have often been in a classroom of unruly first graders who quickly come to attention to join in a chanted count of objects. Part of the excitement is seeing what the final number will be. "Big" numbers seem to have extra power. But children's concept of "big" may be surprising to you. One afternoon my four-year-old asked to have some M&M's close to dinner time. I was reluctant to give them to her, but knowing that a child's idea of "a lot" is different from a grown-up's, I asked, *How many do you want?* She eagerly responded, *Seven!* I agreed, making us both quite happy. By allowing her to choose the number, she felt powerful. If she had chosen too large a number, I would have asked her to choose a smaller one, because I had not agreed to give her any.

LEARN WHAT YOUR CHILD KNOWS, AS WELL AS WHAT SHE DOESN'T KNOW

⚬ ⚬ ⚬ ⚬ ⚬ **Become familiar with your child's** understanding of numbers so that when you work together, you will know what numbers are appropriate to use. You might want to start a notebook (or put a sheet of paper on the refrigerator) in which you record the date and observations of what your child knows. **It may be hard to resist correcting your child, but let her do the thinking and talking**. This cannot be over-emphasized. You need to find out what she knows and needs to learn. Correcting her will interrupt her train of thought and may make her self-conscious about working with you. Notice her errors. Later on you will use the information you gathered to know how high to count or what size numbers to add. You should make sure that she hears the correct numbers and sequence many times.

FIND OUT WHAT YOUR CHILD KNOWS ABOUT SAYING NUMBERS IN THE RIGHT ORDER

⚬ ⚬ ⚬ ⚬ ⚬ **Begin by finding out how high** your child can recite the counting numbers. Have her count aloud without any prompting and without counting objects. If your child can count past 20, notice if she hesitates at numbers after which there are transitions, like 19, 29, and 39. Is she trying to remember what comes next, or is she certain?

Remember or write down the last correct number, but **don't interrupt your child**. If you have a feeling that your child wants help, give it, count together, or take turns counting. Remember the highest number your child knows on her own and record that. You can make a separate entry in your notebook for "can count with help" and record the numbers that you had to supply. If you do this every month, making a careful distinction between what your child can do on her own and what you do to help, you will be as aware of her progress as of her errors.

Use what you learned to help your child

Being familiar with what your child knows tells you what to do next. If your child can count to five, make sure to practice counting to ten, but don't push her to learn the numbers after ten yet. If your child can count to ten, begin to work on the numbers between ten and twenty.

You can watch a video that demonstrates this. Choose the button "There may be more to learn."

www.talkaboutmath.org

When a child can count numbers in the 20s and 30s correctly, another milestone has been reached. For many children, inserting the word "twenty" before the words "one" through "nine" in numbers such as "**twenty**-one," "**twenty**-two," "**twenty**-three . . ." causes them to lose track of their place within the sequence. Children must know the count from one to nine very firmly and notice its role in counting beyond twenty. Keeping the one-through-nine pattern in mind while inserting an additional number word, "twenty," adds another level of difficulty.

If your child is uncertain about what follows 29, 39, 49, etc., count by tens together so that the order of the words "ten," "twenty," "thirty," and so on, becomes familiar. Count piles of objects totaling about 100. You can use pennies, blocks, paper clips, or any other convenient object. You can entertain yourself with your child beside you by trying to guess how many are in the group before you count. Say your guess aloud and then, after counting, comment on how well you think you did. This helps your child to see that when we estimate, we do not expect to get the exact number. It eases some of the pressure to always have the one right answer to a math question. These ideas will become important in her future math.

ONE-TO-ONE COUNTING— CONNECTING EXACTLY ONE NUMBER WORD TO EACH OBJECT TO BE COUNTED

● ● ● ● ● **To count objects,** we must attach one number to each object, and each object must be counted exactly once. This is referred to as "one-to-one counting." A child must be able to count one-to-one before any arithmetic can be understood. When you chant number songs that involve touching one finger or toe as each number is said, you are demonstrating one-to-one counting. Model one-to-one counting by moving objects as you count them. Don't get upset when your child counts the same object over again, says the numbers out of order, or makes up number names—"eleventeen, twelveteen," and "twenty-nine, twenty-ten" are common errors. These are all normal for children learning this complex system. Count together so that she hears the sequence correctly.

Here is a surprising fact: when a child can count five objects accurately, it does not mean that she can count twelve objects. It seems to us that once a person knows that each object must be counted exactly once, it holds true for any amount, but that is not the case. It is usual for a child to first learn one-to-one counting of a small number of objects but to lose track of the count when there are more objects. After one-to-one counting is generally understood, she is still likely to make errors in counting amounts in the teens or over 20. It is hard to remember to say the next number as well as to keep track. If your child is aware of losing track of the count, suggest moving the objects to a new location as each one is counted. Children who are ready for one-to-one counting and understand the need to keep track appreciate the suggestion if it is offered in a friendly manner and quickly adopt this method. Even though your child may have seen you keeping track while counting objects, it is not until the significance of doing so is meaningful to her that she adopts this method herself.

Is all of this more work than you remembered? When you are aware of the complexity, it is easier to be sympathetic and patient while your child learns. It is important to listen to your child while she is counting, just to observe, without correcting every time.

FIND OUT HOW MANY OBJECTS YOUR CHILD CAN COUNT

Give your child some objects to count. Does she know to say one number for each object, or are some objects counted more than once, or some numbers said without being attached to an object? Again, you may have to use self-control to resist telling her to move the objects while counting. You can do that afterwards, but first find how many objects your child can correctly count one-to-one. If she cannot count the amount you give her, try a smaller amount the next time. She may be able to count accurately to 7 but may get mixed up when there are 23 objects in the pile. This is normal for young children. Just see what you can find out about what your child knows so far.

You can watch a video that demonstrates this. Choose the button "Learning to count is hard work" and then "Help your child learn to count."

www.talkaboutmath.org

Use what you learned to help your child

Ask your child to count amounts that are a little larger than the number she counts accurately. Gradually expand the number of objects that she can count and make sure that she knows the names and order of the larger numbers. It is usual for a child to begin to understand the need to count just one object at a time around age 5½, but it still takes time to learn to do so accurately.

THE ORDER IN WHICH WE COUNT DOES NOT AFFECT THE TOTAL

● ● ● ● ● **While the order in which we say** the numbers is important, the order in which we count objects to find the total does not. Here is yet another aspect of counting that children need to learn. Some young children seem to think that the numbers are like names. They always start at the same finger as if the numbers were the names of the fingers. Because numbers are used in so many different contexts to count different things, children eventually understand the idea of quantity instead of names. Make sure to change the order in which you count a group so she will learn this, too.

CONSERVATION OF NUMBER— THE AMOUNT STAYS THE SAME WHEN OBJECTS ARE REARRANGED

The awareness that a group of objects contains the same number of objects even if it is moved around is called "conservation of number." If your child counts a group of objects and gets different amounts each time, it is important to observe whether or not this troubles her. If it doesn't, try having her count fewer objects. A child may be able to conserve a group of 3 objects but not a group of 27. This is a very difficult thing for grown-ups to realize; it seems to us that once the child knows that the number of objects stays the same, the idea should be understood for any size group.

FIND OUT IF YOUR CHILD CAN CONSERVE NUMBERS

When a group of objects is rearranged, does your child know the quantity has not changed? Is this true for a large number of objects as well as a small one? These questions may seem silly, because we know so well that a pile of 65 objects that is rearranged in front of us still has 65 objects if none are added or removed. For most four-year-olds, this is not obvious even with five objects. A group that is spread out seems to contain more than one that is close together. Arrange five pennies or other small objects in a line in front of you and another five with the same spacing in front of your child. Have her count how many you each have and ask if you both have the same amount. If your child says no, continue to practice counting small sets and talking about "the same amount," "more," and "less" until those concepts have meaning. Wait until she understands this idea before trying this next experiment. If your child knows you both have the same amount, spread your pennies further apart but leave hers as they are. Then ask, *Do we have the same amount now?*

If your child looks at you as if you are crazy when you ask this question, you can be pretty sure that she can conserve. If she recounts the pile to find out, conservation is still somewhat uncertain. If your child seems to be wavering in answering, you can offer the chance to count. If she does not want to recount, she probably is nearly sure that both of you have the same amount. In this situation too, you will need to keep your opinion to yourself while you work. If your child needs to count or is certain you have more, she does not yet conserve numbers, but be patient. With experience, she will. If your child was certain that the number of pennies stayed the same, repeat the experiment with more than 30 objects to see if she has the idea for all amounts.

Jean Piaget was a Swiss scientist who conducted many experiments to learn about the development of children's thinking. The method he used to determine whether a child can conserve quantity is probably his most famous experiment.

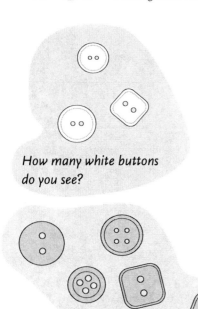

How many white buttons do you see?

Now *how many white buttons?*

Use what you learned to help your child

To give more practice conserving numbers, give your child three white buttons to count. Then place those three white buttons with a few gray buttons and ask how many white buttons there are. (Make sure your child sees that you are using only the white buttons she has already counted and knows these color names.) Add another gray button and repeat the question: *How many white buttons are there?* If your child thinks you are being silly, she can conserve the amount three. Repeat the process, starting with four white buttons until she can hold four in her mind. If three confuses her, start again using only one white button until she thinks it's a silly question, then move to two white buttons.

OTHER WAYS TO COUNT

When your child has learned to count to five, count backwards sometimes. This skill will be important for subtraction and, many years later, for working with signed (negative and positive) numbers. There are songs and chants that count backwards. When you make up your own version of *One little, two little, three little toesies* . . . you can include a verse, *Ten little, nine little, eight little toesies* . . .

It is often useful to count objects by twos, fives, or tens. Children learn the chant of this count long before they understand its use. Many children, when asked to count by twos, will move one object at a time as they say, *two, four, six* . . . Children can recite the chant without understanding its relation to quantity. You will need to demonstrate the meaning and allow your child to practice many times before this is fully understood.

RECOGNIZING WRITTEN NUMBERS

● ● ● ● ● **Notice that so far** I have made no mention of written numbers. Recognition of the symbols 0–9 is one more skill that a young child must master. It is separate from knowing the names of the numbers and understanding the quantity represented by each digit. You can help by pointing out written numbers wherever they occur and saying the numbers that they represent. This skill is somewhat like learning to recognize the letters of the alphabet. However, while a child who learns the name of a letter has a long way to go before being able to read words, a child who has been saying and using numbers can immediately link a written number to an already familiar idea because the number symbols each represent a number word.

Songs with backwards counting

"Ten Little Frogs"
by Louise B. Scott and Virginia Pavelko

<u>Ten</u> green and speckled frogs
Sat on a speckled log
Eating some most delicious bugs.
Yum, yum!

One jumped into the pool
Where it was nice and cool
Then there were <u>nine</u> green
speckled frogs

<u>Nine</u> green and speckled frogs . . .

Glub, glub!

● ● ● ● ●

There were <u>ten</u> in the bed
And the little one said,
Roll over! Roll over!
So they all rolled over
And one fell out.

There were <u>nine</u> in the bed,
And the little one said . . .

[until one finally has the bed to herself:
There was <u>one</u> in the bed,
And the little one said, *Hooray!]*

● ● ● ● ●

<u>Ten</u> little monkeys jumping on the bed
One fell off and bumped her head
Momma called the doctor and the
doctor said,
*No more monkeys jumping
on the bed!*

<u>Nine</u> little monkeys jumping on the bed
One fell off and bumped her head . . .

1

2

3

4

5

You can make a set of number cards using 3×5 index cards. I usually cut them in half to make them easy to handle. I use a very large font size and print them on my computer. You can make them more fun by pasting wallpaper or wrapping paper on the back. Use the same pattern for the back of all the cards so that your child will memorize the numbers and not the design or color that accompanies them. A set of cards for the numbers 1–20 can serve many purposes. A youngster can be asked to put the numbers 1–5 in order. Later you will give her 1–10 and eventually 1–20 to put in order. Before she is able to put them in order herself, you will count them and place them together. While making dinner, you can put cucumber slices on plates and ask her to find the number card that matches the total number of slices on each plate. Again, you might start with the numbers 1–3 and increase the quantity as she learns to count accurately and recognizes the number symbols. Use your knowledge of her number sense to guide you. While this activity might sound too much like school, your child wants your attention and wants you to do things with her. Sometimes you will pose the questions and at other times she will. If you are having fun and don't get upset by mistakes, your child will be happy to participate.

Another way to have your child see the numbers is as points spaced at equal distances along a "number line." This is useful for many mathematical concepts. It demonstrates the order of the numbers and the equal distance between them. The line can be traveled forwards or backwards, corresponding to addition or subtraction. You can use adding machine paper to make the line with your child. She will see how you make use of an object or a ruler to help you space the numbers at regular distances.

You might also make a version in which you place the numbers far enough apart for her to walk along the line. Sidewalk chalk or numbers scratched in dirt could be used to do this outdoors.

DON'T DESPAIR IF THE LEARNING CURVE IS NOT SMOOTH

● ● ● ● ● **All the counting ideas and skills** discussed in this chapter are developing as you plan counting experiences with your child. Sometimes a child will seem to know something and then forget it or be unsure the next time you count. Sometimes the learning will jump ahead with several different ideas grasped at once. Although the ideas are listed in a progressive sequence, your child's understanding will not necessarily develop in this order. There are times your child will go forward, then back again before she has solid understanding. Make sure you choose activities that you both enjoy, stay patient, and count!

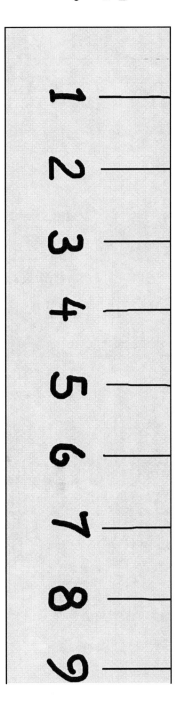

A number line. Notice that the numbers are placed at the lines rather than in the spaces between lines.

Important ideas from chapter 1 for you to think about

▼

Count many things in a variety of contexts—small groups and large ones.

Learning to count is complex. It requires:

- memorizing the names of the numbers

- saying them in order

- associating one number with one object (one-to-one correspondence)

- recognizing the patterns involved in the names of the numbers greater than 20

- understanding that the last number said represents the quantity in the whole group

- knowing that the order in which we count objects does not affect the total

- realizing that the same number of objects are present when the objects are rearranged (conservation)

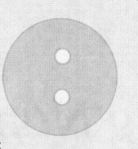

It is also helpful to:

- picture the numbers as equidistant points on a "number line"

- count by tens

- count backwards

- count by twos

Remember that recognizing the written numbers is a separate skill from counting.

▲

Find out what your child knows and use that information to choose the next activity.

Counting is the beginning of your math relationship with your child—keep it fun and friendly.

2

Collecting Numbers

Statistics

—————————●—●—————————

Before we move to traditional arithmetic, let's look at other branches of math that lend themselves to practical and fun family activities. We'll begin with one that we experience daily: statistics. Children are exposed to statistics from the moment they are born. When the pediatrician tells us the child's percentiles for height and weight, these numbers can provide clues to the infant's health because information has been collected from large numbers of babies.

WHAT IS STATISTICS?

Statistics is the branch of mathematics that deals with the collection and analysis of numerical data. It uses numbers to tell us about the world around us. It is impossible to open a newspaper without encountering statistics in the form of graphs, percentages, charts, and tables, or embedded in the articles. Many people skip these aspects of the articles, leaving them with an imperfect understanding. To allow children to grow up as full participants in society, start them off with age-appropriate data collection and lead them to more sophisticated understanding.

A FAMILY EXPLORATION

● ● ● ● ● **One winter my children** became enamored of clementines, a type of small mandarin orange. After we'd eaten some, the younger one asked, *Does every clementine have the same number of pieces?* Her question was about both statistics and science and led me to wonder: do all clementines have the same number of segments? How many are there? Is the number of pieces always odd or always even? None of us knew the answers, so we posted a strip of paper on the refrigerator and agreed not to eat a clementine without first counting the pieces and recording the number on the paper. Because there are not many segments in an orange, this provides good practice in one-to-one counting. The number of pieces in the orange is the last number said in the count. Writing the numbers is another experience in hearing a number and seeing its written representation. All of these basic understandings and skills can be developed as you do this simple activity.

By creating a list of numbers of segments in the oranges we ate, we soon found out that there was

> ### Writing numbers backwards
>
> Don't worry if your child writes numbers (or letters) in reverse. This is normal for children through age six. Handwriting practice should be separate from learning mathematics. Make sure your child knows he counted correctly; you don't want to confuse mathematical knowledge with the muscle and eye-hand control needed to avoid writing backwards or illegibly.

Do all oranges contain the same number of segments?

a variation in the number of pieces. We knew the range—the smallest and largest numbers of segments and how far apart these are. We could also see that

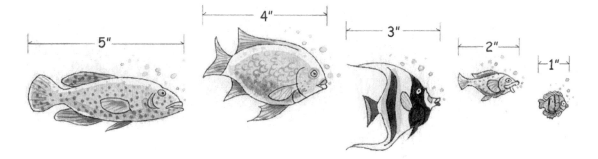

These fish range in size from one inch to five inches.
We can also say they have a range of four inches
from the shortest to the longest.

some numbers occurred much more often than others. We were all learning together, since none of us knew what the results would be.

BEGINNING TO LEARN THE MEANING OF "AVERAGE"

We will talk about other kinds of averages in volume 2.

The more data we collected, the better sense we had of the possible number of pieces in one clementine. This relates to the sophisticated idea of average. When we need an average, we are looking for one number that is a good representation of a group of different numbers. An activity such as this one, of collecting information and talking about the findings, is an excellent way to help children become comfortable with numbers and to prepare them for understanding more difficult kinds of averages. For young children, the only type of average that is meaningful is "mode"—the number that occurs most often.

COLLECT INFORMATION ABOUT YOUR ENVIRONMENT

• • • • • **Find many things** that can be counted and keep a record of them. Fruits such as apples, grapefruits, and oranges are useful for this purpose because you can count the seeds. If you go to the beach, collect shells. Sort them by type and see how many there are of each type. Count the stripes in their designs. Put out a bird feeder and see what kinds of birds visit and the number of each kind. In the park or your backyard, count the number of petals on daisies, asters, or other common plants.

Seashells can be sorted by type, even though no two are exactly the same.

Notice that sorting plays a role here. As we distinguish between types of oranges, birds, or shells, sorting expands our understanding of the world. The classification of the natural world is a type of sorting, a topic that you might not think of as part of math.

If your children eat candy, let them have the little bags and see if every bag of M&M's contains the same quantity. M&M's come in a variety of colors whose quantities can be compared. You can count the number of raisins in small boxes. Do they each contain the same amount? Why might differences occur? Count how many people are in line at the grocery store. Are there days or times that the lines are shorter? Why do you think this happens? How many cars go by before your bus comes? The number of cars parked along your street can be counted on different days and recorded. Are there different numbers

In the next chapter we will discuss sorting with regard to language acquisition and measurement.

on different days or at different times? What might be the reasons for this?

Observations about data can lead to creative thinking and also to hypothesizing—making reasonable guesses. In many cases there will be no precise answer. While mathematics is generally associated with exactness, this is a field in which you can experience math freely, without that restraint. Maybe there are no cars on the block today because work is going to be done on the pavement, or maybe it's because a movie will be filmed there, or maybe it's mid-week and everyone is at work. You can make up silly reasons. There is no right or wrong in thinking up these possibilities. Some can be checked (Is there a "No Parking Today" sign that gives a reason?) and for some you'll accept what seems the most reasonable explanation as you continue to observe and gather more data.

ESTIMATION

Sometimes we cannot know the exact answer to our questions but can get a good approximation. Many methods of estimating require more advanced mathematics than we are talking about here, so we will not discuss ways to estimate how many leaves are on a tree or hairs on a head. There are some interesting questions that we can use to find a ballpark figure by counting, adding, and guessing, such as the number of people living in a small apartment building or on a block of houses.

Data collected over time can provide information about a single person, plant, pet, city, or weather system. It can show change:

>*How much did I grow this year?*
>
>*How tall will I be when I grow up? Will I be taller than my brother?*
>
>*How much does a plant grow in one week? (Bean plants are good for this because they grow quickly.)*
>
>*How much does my pet weigh each month? (What does the vet say about my pet's weight and health?)*
>
>*What is the temperature today? What was it yesterday? What is predicted for tomorrow?*

Growth is a concern of most children. Many families keep track of a child's height by marking a spot on the wall and labeling it with the child's name and date. In this way, your child can see a representation of his growth. You can also keep track of the growth of a plant or the weight of a pet. Write these on a strip of paper posted where you will find it again.

I bet I'm a lot taller!

An activity that also helps children learn to read two-digit numbers is keeping track of the temperature. Unlike growth, this might change daily, making it something that can be recorded more frequently, adding to the interest and continuity. If your list contains the date as well as the temperature, this can also be an opportunity for your child to become familiar with the calendar and a graph. Remember that in order for comparisons to be meaningful, it is important to check the temperature at nearly the same time each day.

See how many different types of data you can count and study. These collections are an informal way to develop ease in using numbers to understand the world around us. They also provide contexts in which to practice counting. Keeping a record and finding meaning in the numbers is what statisticians do. You and your child can do this together.

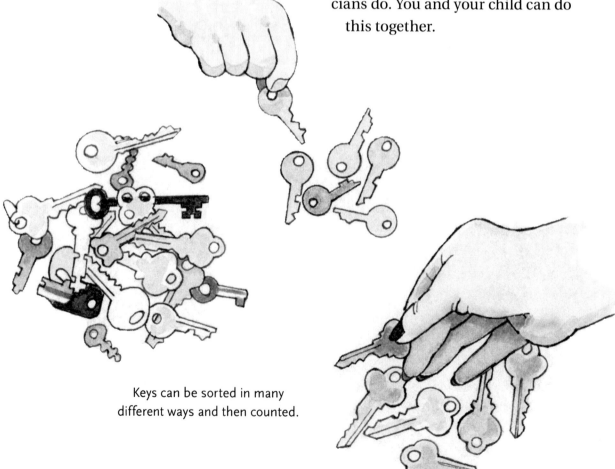

Keys can be sorted in many different ways and then counted.

Important ideas from chapter 2 for you to think about

▼ ▲

Use statistics to explore the natural world.

Make collections of toys and natural objects for counting, practicing comparative language about the sizes of the groups, and increasing vocabulary.

▲ ▼

Get comfortable with not knowing the answers to some of your child's questions, and use them as an opportunity to explore together.

3

Measurement
Logic and Language

● ● ●

Measurement provides many natural math activities because you use it daily. It gives you opportunities to work in different branches of math: when we measure how many blocks tall we are, we count; older children see the meaning of fractions and decimals when we measure with rulers or meter sticks; area and volume measurement are part of geometry; I am delighted when first and second graders proudly use negative numbers as part of discussions of winter temperatures.

The possibilities are enormous and, because you use measurement frequently, it is likely to be the most comfortable math you do.

TYPES OF MEASUREMENT

● ● ● ● ● **When the term "measurement" is used**, many people think of linear measurement first—that is, lines that can be measured with a ruler. Children are familiar with linear measurement of their heights at the doctor's office and with lines on the wall to mark growth. They may see you use a yardstick to determine whether a piece of furniture will fit into a new location.

Children also have some experience with the measurement of time. This includes counting how many years old they are, days until special events occur, or minutes until bedtime.

When we measure length and time, we generally use standard units: inches, feet, and miles, or centimeters, meters, and kilometers for length; seconds, minutes, days, and years, for time.

There are also measurements that use nonstandard units, such as paces to get an idea of the dimensions of a room, prices at different stores, grades students receive in different classes.

The next two pages contain a list of common types of measurement and some of the contexts in which these are used. It is intended to make you aware of how many types of measurement you make so that you can include your children when measuring.

COMMON MEASUREMENTS

What We Measure	Contexts in Which We Measure It	Units of Measurement	Relative Measurement
Time	calendar	days, weeks, months, seasons,	natural days, position of the sun
	day	seconds, minutes, hours	earlier, later, shorter, longer
	periods within the day	bedtime, mealtime	
	age	years, decades	
	history	years, decades, centuries, millennia	eras
	cooking	seconds, minutes, hours	
	sports	minutes per game (basketball) fractions of seconds (races)	innings (baseball)
	music	beats per minute beats per measure	slower, faster
Temperature	body temperature cooking weather swimming, bathing room fish tank refrigerator	degrees Celsius and/or Fahrenheit (C°,F°)	warmer, cooler, too hot, just right, too cold
Weight	body (human, animal) food object	ounces, pounds, tons grams, kilograms	
	paper	pounds per ream	
	fabric		light-, heavyweight
	mail for postage	ounces, pounds	
	luggage	pieces, pounds	
	road and bridge loads	tons	safe for travel
	elevator	pounds, numbers of people	

What We Measure	Contexts in Which We Measure It	Units of Measurement	Relative Measurement
Length (width, depth)	distance	inch, foot, yard, mile centimeter, meter, kilometer	nearer, farther
	height: human building animal (horse)	inches, feet; meters stories; feet hands	shorter, taller
	plant	inches, feet	
	sports (football)	yards	
	fabric	yards	
	room	feet	
	object	inches, feet; centimeters, meters	smaller, bigger
	knitting	stitches	
Area	room, apartment, office, house	square feet	smaller, bigger, larger
	land	acres, square miles	
	wall (for paint or wallpaper)	gallons or rolls	
Volume	air in a room (for an air-conditioner)	cubic feet, cubic meters	
Capacity	container	pint, quart, gallon	smaller, larger
	refrigerator	cubic feet	
Pulse	body	beats per minute	slower, faster
Food energy	diet	calories	
Angle	plumb line camera lens	degrees	pointy, wide
Noise	quality-of-life environmental issues	decibels	softer, louder

WHAT IS COMMON TO ALL THESE TYPES OF MEASUREMENT?

What all measurements have in common is that they select one attribute of an object and assign a number to it. In order to measure we must be able to select one characteristic of an object and a unit that has that same characteristic and make a comparison. Young children laugh at the story of Amelia Bedelia when she uses a tape measure to measure "one cup of rice." They already appreciate the need to measure the appropriate attribute. When we measure how long it takes us to travel between home and school, we measure the time spent traveling by looking at the change in time shown on our watches. If we say that it took twenty minutes to get to school, we know nothing about the distance. We need to know some other factors, like whether we walked or drove. We know nothing about whether the time went quickly with laughter or dragged on in uncomfortable silence. In baking, the same one-half cup measure can be used for milk, flour, or berries. Volume is just one of many characteristics.

ATTRIBUTES: NOTICING MUST PRECEDE MEASUREMENT

Noticing the attributes of objects is part of the important work of childhood and is a necessary part of language acquisition. Toddlers are constantly doing this as they decide, for example, what makes something a chair, what is not a chair, and what is sort of a chair. Children ask many questions about the categories they observe. Some of these we find astute, some make us laugh, and sometimes we get tired of being asked so many questions! As we discuss classification, we develop a sense of logic, which is vital to mathematics, coherent conversations, writing, and many other life skills.

We can help children focus on the attributes of objects by playing games with common household objects. A button or lid collection (save all non-sharp jar and bottle tops) is excellent for this purpose. You will also need a circle of string, a sheet of paper, or a plate. The string (or paper, or plate) will provide a way to distinguish between those objects that share a chosen attribute and those that do not. Look at the buttons together and see how many different characteristics you can find. Don't limit your categories to color. Some may be bumpy and some smooth. Some have one, two, or four holes. Some have a single loop in the back, some have holes through the center. Some are round, some square, and some have other shapes. They may be big and small. Just talking about and sorting buttons together is a good first activity. You can begin the sorting game by saying, *Let's find all the buttons that are _____.* These buttons can be placed in the circle. Use this as an opportunity to expand vocabulary. Little children are very observant. They will probably find some categories you did not notice. Be sure to let them know they have impressed you. A pleasure of parenting can be learning from your child as well as helping your child learn from you.

Common objects that make good collections for sorting

keys

buttons

jar lids

toy vehicles

toy animals

toy characters

stones

shells

AN ATTRIBUTE GUESSING GAME

Once you and your child are familiar with your button collection, you can play a guessing game that strengthens your child's observation skills.

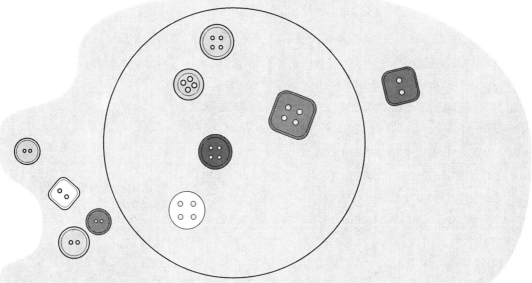

The buttons with four holes go inside the circle.
All the other buttons stay outside.

Each of you should take a handful of buttons or lids. Without saying what you have chosen, put all your metal buttons, for example, into the circle. Ask your child if she can guess what characteristic you have chosen. If she thinks she knows, have her add her matching ones to the circle. If there are several players, no one should say what they think the rule is, but they should ask, *Does this belong?* as pieces are added to the circle. Young children think that a match means an exact match of all attributes. They think they should find exact copies of the metal buttons you placed in the circle. So include many different metal buttons in the group before inviting her to put some in. It takes a while before children feel comfortable using just one or two attributes. If a child puts a button in the circle that is not metal, you should ask what attribute she was thinking of. Perhaps, without your realizing it, you chose all buttons that have four holes and she has also chosen one with four holes. In that case, accept her category and acknowledge that she noticed something you missed. Then you can ask if she can figure out what you had noticed about all of the buttons you chose. If possible, show her a non-metal button with four holes that you did not include in the set. The non-included buttons are important clues in this game. When you are fairly sure that the attribute has been identified, have her name it—metal! You can also make a label for the circle, incorporating a pre-reading skill. This activity strengthens your child's use of logic as you decide which objects are inside the chosen group (such as "the metal buttons") and which are outside.

After you have started the game with you choosing the attribute, invite your child to begin one. At first, she may copy what you did, or put together buttons with no common characteristics. If she copied you, ask her to find another group of buttons. If she seems to have just put in random buttons, find a group together, by asking her to tell you what she notices about some of those she put in. Then ask her to find all the buttons that have one of the characteristics she mentions. She might put in too few buttons for you to know what type of buttons she chose. Thinking out loud, say, *I wonder if you were thinking of all the two-hole buttons, but I see that there are still some buttons with two holes in your pile that you didn't put into the center.* This might help her to realize she's made an error and needs to add some buttons.

> The wording
> *I wonder if you were thinking . . . but . . .*
> can serve as a model for handling errors in many different situations.

The main point of this simple version of the game is to establish categories. When you create the label for the set, make sure that everyone agrees on the wording. Is it clear enough so that you can tell which buttons belong in the set and which do not? An example is to say, *All the buttons in the circle are squares. All the buttons we left out of the circle are not squares.* Are there some buttons for which it is hard to decide? If so, can the wording be changed so that you can decide more easily? An example might be changing "blue buttons" to "all-blue buttons" so that partially blue buttons are excluded. Another change could be "buttons that have blue on them" so that all partially blue buttons are included. Perhaps your child would like to make the label. The joint decision-making develops logic and language while you work in partnership to make the decision. The same circle can be reused to designate another set like "large buttons." The labels can later be used as part of a reading game in which the child tries to remember what each label says.

Making the attribute game more challenging

When this game gets easy, you can play with buttons that share two attributes, like round buttons with one hole. You should introduce this by letting your child know that the game is about to get more difficult. There would still be one circle in which to place buttons. If the child only notices one of the attributes, like "round", you will have to find a round button with more than one hole that you did not include in the set. Show that to her and tell her that, while round is part of your idea, there is something else to look for. In this way

you acknowledge the part that she did figure out and
encourage her to look further.

This is not the place to try to trick your child. When the
game seems too easy to be fun, make it more difficult.
As the game becomes more challenging, talk about
the new rules. Make sure that they are clear. You can
play an "open round" in which you discuss individual
buttons and why they do or do not meet the criteria.
Such a discussion increases your child's vocabulary
as well as logical thinking. It is likely that your child
will try to trick you, perhaps by not putting all the
square buttons in the circle, even though her criteria is
"square buttons." It is likely that she feels troubled and
wants to know something you don't know. You can use
this information to help you play in a way that allows
her to have control over when to stop and when to try
a new version. The new version should include a game
that she makes up. Most children like to create their
own games, but the rules may be hard to follow and
change as you play. Creating a playable game is a great
exercise in logic. Let your child work at this, too.

Adding another challenge: two overlapping circles with a label for each

This is quite difficult for many adults. The temptation
is to create, for example, a circle for "white" and an
overlapping circle for "red" and to place pink buttons
in the intersection. While it is true in the world of
colored glass that an overlap of white and red will
create pink, we are now creating sets of objects for
which things clearly either do or do not belong. If one

circle has the label "white," then everything that is placed within it must be something that we would call "white," and similarly for the circle "red." There is nothing that would fit into the intersection of these two categories unless we change the labels to something like "partly white" and "partly red." When the circles contain two aspects of the same attribute (in the example here, both were colors), the way to have elements belong in the intersection is to find a complex wording that means "only partly this way." A better way to create sets with members that belong in the overlapped section is to use two different attributes. An example is to make one circle "white" and another "two holes."

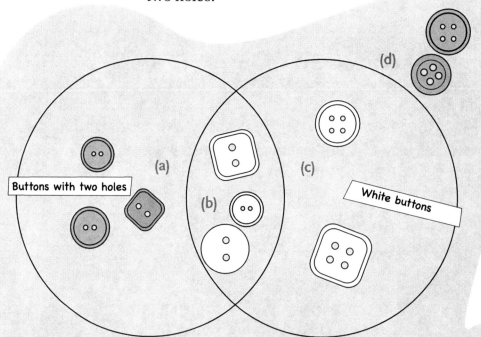

When two circles overlap, there are places for four categories of objects. Here, one circle represents "buttons with two holes" and the other circle contains "white buttons." This means

    (a) non-white buttons with two holes go in the "buttons with two holes," but outside of the intersection of the two circles

    (b) any white buttons that have two holes are placed in the intersection of the two circles

    (c) all white buttons belong in the "white buttons" circle

    (d) buttons that are not white and do not have two holes go outside the two circles.

In this way, all buttons within the "buttons with two holes" circle have two holes, and all buttons within the "white buttons" circle will be white. The overlapping section will be for buttons that are both white and have two holes. It will not receive a separate label because the already existing labels, "white" and "two holes," both apply to this intersection. This is because two different characteristics were used: "color" and "number of holes." If you created two circles using the same characteristic, the meaning of intersection would not be clear because the intersection would need its own label. For example, if both circles were about "color," the intersection of "blue" and "red" would be "purple," a new group that we don't think of as belonging to "blue" or "red." When you use two different attributes, the intersection can be named by joining the two labels with "and." In the button example above, the intersection is "buttons that are white **and** have two holes." Experiment with combinations of labels. Always check to see that everything within one circle belongs to that group.

> This branch of math is "set theory" or "Boolean algebra." It includes graphs called Venn diagrams that show the intersections of sets.

RELATIVE MEASUREMENT

● ● ● ● ● **Once children understand** how to focus on one attribute at a time, they can be asked to place objects in order, from smallest to largest. When we do this, we do not assign a specific measurement number. Instead we notice relative sizes. Young children can be given sticks of varying length to place in order by size. A simple version can be made with straws or sticks. It is important to use materials, such as drinking straws, that are straight and that have the same width and color for all the pieces.

Straws are easy to cut for placing in size order.

Three sticks will be enough for a beginning game. Later you can add more. This activity, too, is as much a part of language as of math. Vocabulary may include "shorter," "shortest," "longer," "longest," "taller," and "tallest." These are linear measurements.

See pp. 155 to 165.

You will also help your child compare areas, volumes, and weights. For area, cut graduated sizes of the same shape.

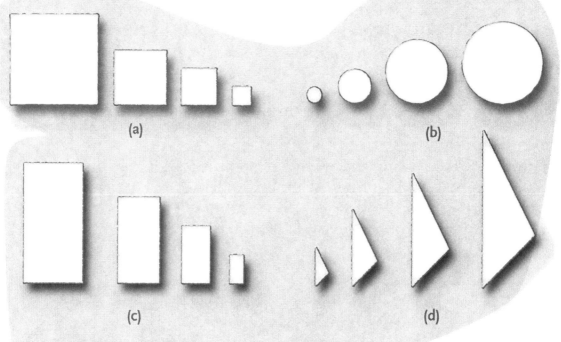

(a) All squares are similar.
(b) All circles are similar.
(c) Similar rectangles have sides that are proportional.
(d) Similar triangles have the same angles and sides that are proportional.

You will not ask your children to compare the areas of different shapes. This is too difficult. You can cut squares, circles, triangles, rectangles. For all of these, use the same material and color so that only the size varies. If you cut triangles or rectangles, you must make sure that they are all similar to each other. That is, the sides must all be in the same ratio. If a rectangle is 2″ × 4″ then another can be 3″ × 6″ and a third can be 4″ × 8″. All of these have sides in the ratio of 1 to 2. In other words, the length is twice the width. To make different size triangles, you can use the corners of a piece of paper to make right triangles with legs of equal length or proportional lengths.

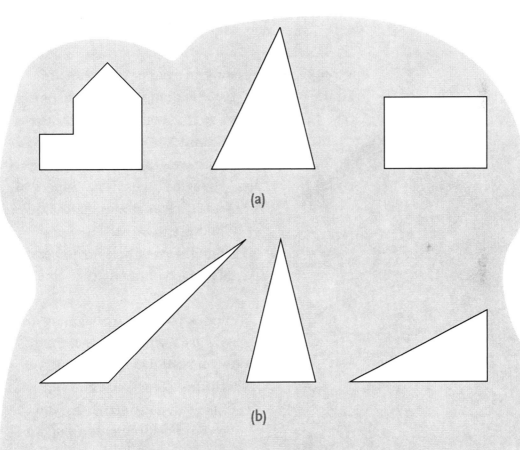

(a)

(b)

Things that are too hard for young children to compare:
  (a) Different shapes are too hard to compare. These three shapes all have the same area, but a child is likely to think that the tallest one has the largest area.
  (b) Non-similar shapes are too hard to compare. Even though these three figures are all triangles, it is difficult to see that they have the same area.

Vocabulary of relative area includes "smaller," "smallest," "littler," "littlest," "bigger," "biggest," "larger," "largest." For rectangles we can also use "wider," "widest," "longer," "longest."

Nesting cubes and Russian dolls are toys that are also objects in graduated volumes. We use the same vocabulary as we do for area to compare volumes, but, if it is appropriate to the objects, we can also use "deeper" and "deepest."

For weight comparisons, use paper cups that are partially filled with different amounts of sand or rocks. Cover the cups so that your child cannot see how much sand is in the cup. Words associated with weight are "lighter," "lightest," "heavier," "heaviest." Spherical objects such as stones, balls, and balloons can be used to demonstrate that weight is not necessarily related to volume.

I hope you now realize that you easily use terms of measurement with your child every day. Without acting as a teacher, while you engage in daily activities, you can make measurements aloud and use them to help your child learn math.

The balloon is bigger, but the rock is much heavier!

Important ideas from chapter 3 for you to think about

▲ ▼ ▲

Begin by helping your child look at separate attributes of an object, because all measurements have in common the assignment of a number to an attribute.

Use the vocabulary of relative sizes before assigning specific numbers.

Remember to incorporate these various aspects of measurement in the activities you choose:

- the acquisition of language

- the logic of sorting

- counting

- geometry

▼ ▲ ▼

Include your child in the many ways that you measure every day, even if only by thinking aloud.

4

Measurement

Number Sense and Geometry

After children have worked on relative measurement, they are ready to measure as we do, using numbers. Now they can connect measurement to counting, something we cannot overdo with young children.

ESTIMATING SIZE

Paper clips can be linked in a chain and used for linear measurements such as a child's height, your height, the perimeter (length around the edge) of a table. Paper clips are especially useful because they can be used to measure around a curved surface like the lip of a garbage pail, your head, or a tree trunk. It can be

Relative size measurements such as "shorter, shortest, heavier, heaviest" are discussed in chapter 3, p. 32.

fun to first guess how many paper clips long each object is.

Let your child guess first, since he is likely to be influenced by your number. Some children are reluctant to estimate. They may dislike being wrong and do not understand the difference between estimating and counting. If this is the case, just go ahead and make your estimate out loud. Later say, *I was close* or *That wasn't such a good guess*. In this way he sees you are comfortable with a non-exact answer. Another way to help your child (and yourself) is to link together several paper clips, perhaps five of them, and to look at their length and the length that you are about to measure. Then use that comparison to help you estimate. Even if you multiply, explain your thinking out loud so that your child can begin to learn this estimation method.

Measuring the length of a box in paper clips.

Larger distances can be measured in footsteps. One way to keep children from complaining about the length of a walk is to guess and then count the number of steps it takes to walk one block. This is an activity to do when you will be walking several blocks of the same length. You can only count one person's steps at a time. As the numbers get high, it becomes difficult to say one number per step, and everyone needs to help. (It is also very difficult to count when someone else is counting at a different pace.) I am always amazed at young children's quick grasp of the idea that the larger the person, the fewer steps they will need.

How many steps do we take in one block?

COMPARING SIZES

○ ○ ○ ○ ○ **Children have a difficult time** answering a question that asks how many more there are in one group than in another. Some kindergartners will show you the group that contains more but are unable to make sense of this type of question. Linear measurement helps to make this idea meaningful.

Use two sticks or other objects of different lengths. Ask your child, *Which one is shorter?* After he has correctly identified the shorter stick, say, *Let's measure it to see how many paper clips long it is.* Next, place the longer stick next to the shorter one and the chain of paper clips. Ask, *How many more paper clips do you think we will need to measure this one if we save time and use the chain you already made?* You might both guess how many more will be needed. Then have him add paper clips of a different color (or mark the new clips with masking tape) to the chain to find the length of the longer stick. Make clear statements about these lengths: *The shorter stick was 8 paper clips long. The longer stick was 11 paper clips long. The longer stick was 3 paper clips longer than the shorter one. We needed 3 **more** paper clips to match the longer one.*

The big spoon is three paper clips longer than the smaller spoon. We needed three more paper clips to measure it.

Does he remember the number of clips that were in the shorter chain? Can he count on to find out how many are in the longer chain? Can he answer the question about how many more paper clips were needed to make the longer chain? Or does he need to make two separate chains to measure the sticks? If necessary, form the sentences for him so that he hears the statement while he is looking at the chains. Adding on to the first chain might not yet have the same meaning as beginning from one. This is normal. Your child will understand after he has more experience with these words and ideas.

USING MEASUREMENT TO DEMONSTRATE PLACE VALUE

● ● ● ● ● **Observe your child as he counts.** Is he comfortable using groups of ten? Does he ignore the groups of ten and count each paper clip? He needs many more experiences that help him believe that counting by tens will reach the same number as counting by ones. If there are three groups of ten and four more squares (or paper clips, or Legos), does he know immediately that this is 34, or is he uncertain? Ask him, *Would you like to count by ones to be sure?* If he accepts the offer to count by ones, you will know that he is not yet convinced that thirty is three tens. If he looks at you as if you are being ridiculous, you know that he probably has a good grasp of this relationship. Does he say, *ten, twenty, thirty* as he counts groups of tens and then *forty, fifty* . . . as he counts the ones? This is an indication that he does not yet understand that we say "ten" to mean ten objects and "twenty" to mean ten more objects. If your child does this, count many groups both ways.

We can use informal measurement to find the areas of irregular shapes and to compare the areas of very different shapes. You and your child can create shapes and estimate their areas. Pennies or plastic bottle caps can be used to cover shapes and find out their relative

You will read more about understanding two-digit numbers and place value in chapters 6 and 9, pp. 77 and 120.

areas. For making comparisons, the gaps between them will not be a problem. *Does it take more pennies to cover the squiggly shape or the triangle?* The pennies or caps can be put in groups of ten so that they can be counted singly and by tens and ones.

To find the area of a rectangle, draw rectangles on graph paper or make them from a pack of square candies. Count the number of small squares that fit inside it.

See p. 181.

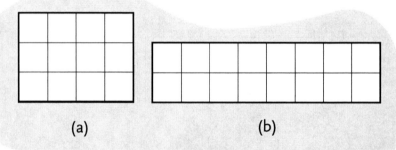

(a)   (b)

The area of rectangle: (a) is 12 squares
(b) is 16 squares

Addition will be discussed thoroughly in chapters 7 and 9, but because it relates closely to rectangle area, it is described here. Areas of rectangles are also useful for seeing the meaning of multiplication. This important third grade topic is discussed in volume 2.

Rectangle area is also an excellent way to build understanding of addition and multiplication. If each row contains the same number of squares, we can repeatedly add that same amount and save time. If your child already has some experience with addition, you might pose the problem: *How can we find the answer without counting all the squares? Can you think of a shortcut?* How does he go about adding? Does he see patterns that he can use to add? If there are two rows of 8, does he see this as two rows of 5 and two rows of 3?

Another quick method is to realize that the first row of 8, plus 2 more from the second row makes 10. With

the 6 other squares in the second row, the total is 16.
Perhaps your child knows from memory that 6 + 6 = 12
and can then count the remaining pairs by twos.
All of these shortcuts use known facts to derive
unknown ones. This is an extremely important addition skill for children to develop.

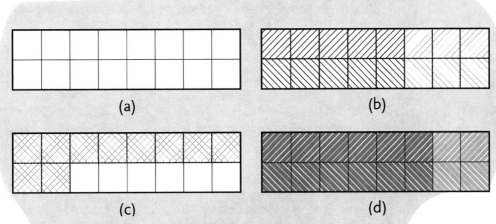

To add two rows of eight, we can look at them in many ways:
  (a) two rows of eight: 8 + 8 = 16
  (b) two rows of (5 + 3) = 10 + 6 = 16
  (c) one row of 8 + 2 more from the next row makes 10, and the 6 more in the second
       row makes 16 in all
  (d) two rows of (6 + 2) = 12 + 4 = 16

MEASURING PERIMETER

● ● ● ● ● **Area and perimeter are confusing**
for many people. I tell children that perimeter is the
length an ant walks around the edge of a shape and
area is a way to measure how much space a shape covers. Chains of paper clips can be used to measure the
perimeters of a variety of shapes. It can be surprising
to realize that the same perimeter can enclose very
different areas. Test this out with your child. Link the

ends of your paper clip chain to form a circle. Find its area by filling the circle with same-size objects, such as pennies or bottle tops. Without breaking the links, use the same chain to form a skinny rectangle and measure its area. How do they compare? Try some other shapes. Then make a different size paper clip chain and use it to compare the areas of a circle, skinny rectangle and other shapes. *What shape has the largest area for a fixed number of paper clips?*

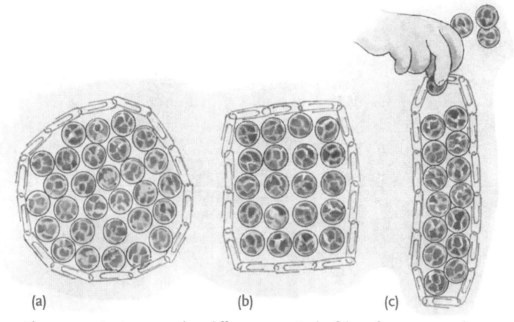

(a)　　　　　　　　　(b)　　　　　　　　(c)

The same perimeter can enclose different areas. Each of these figures was made with 14 paper clips.

    (a) In a circle, 14 paper clips hold 29 pennies.

    (b) In a wide rectangle, 14 paper clips hold 20 pennies.

    (c) In a skinny rectangle, 14 paper clips hold only 15 pennies.

Create different shapes that have the same area. For example, you can use 12 paper squares or 50 beans to form different shapes. Do all the same-area shapes have the same perimeter? Remember to make many irregular shapes, not only the usual ones, like rectangles.

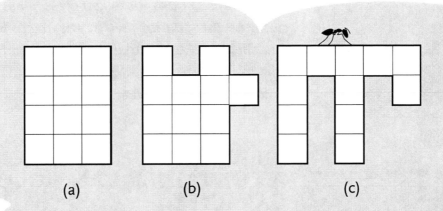

(a)   (b)   (c)

Figures with the same area can have different perimeters. Here are three shapes, each made with an area of 12 squares. Each one has a different perimeter (the length of a walk around the outside of the figure):

(a) perimeter = 14
(b) perimeter = 18
(c) perimeter = 26

Notice that I am not suggesting that you measure the perimeter using string which you then compare to a ruler. This is too abstract for a young child. We are keeping to things that he can count. However, you might try using strings to compare two different perimeters to see which is longer. Pay attention to how your child does this. After you remove the string from the shape, straighten it into a line and ask, *Is it the same length as the edge of the shape?* If he is not sure, it is not helpful to use this method to compare lengths. Sometimes a perimeter can be much greater than we expected when seen in this way. Remember that you are doing this to learn about your child's thinking, not in order to tell him how to answer your questions. If he is not yet conserving length, you now know that he needs many more experiences. Find opportunities to guess, then measure, the lengths of a variety of objects.

For example, *I think the height of this chair is the same as the height of the toy shelf in your room.* You can place a rubber band as a marker on a broom handle and use that to compare these lengths. Comment on how close or far off your guess was.

MEASURING HOW MUCH A CONTAINER CAN HOLD: CAPACITY

Lego bricks that are all the same size, beads, or beans can be used to measure the capacity of differently shaped containers. You might guess the number of objects that a container will hold and then fill it. If you use Legos, dump them in loosely—you do not need to be very accurate—and in this way, the numbers will be smaller and the container can be filled quickly. To connect this activity to the meaning of the tens and ones places in two-digit numbers, before counting the objects, stack the Legos in tens (or put the other objects in piles of ten). Count the objects in tens and ones. Does your child believe that the amount is the same when you count this way as when you count by ones?

MEASURING VOLUME

In addition to estimation and counting, the containers and beans can also be used to compare sizes. Use a shallow container and a tall, narrow one. Ask your child, *Which do you think will hold more? How can we find out without having to count? Which container should I fill first?* Is your child able to make a

> If you use beads or beans, you can put ten in each section of an egg carton.

> The difference between capacity and volume: Capacity tells us how much a container can hold. A one-quart milk carton can hold one quart of milk. Technically, the volume of the carton is measured by flattening it and seeing the amount of cardboard used to make it, but both words are used to mean how much a container can hold.

plan? One plan might be to fill one container and then to pour the beans from it into the other one. What do the results tell you?

The ability to conserve volume takes a while to develop. Take two identical shallow containers and fill them to the same point. Then pour the contents of one of these into a tall, narrow one. Place the original filled shallow container next to the newly filled tall one that now holds the same amount. Ask your child, *Which container has more in it?* Remember that you are doing this to inform yourself about your child's level of understanding. If he does not yet know that the two amounts are the same, this only means that you will give your child many more similar experiences. If you feel disappointed at him for not knowing, do your best to hide it. Otherwise, he will quickly sense your feeling, and find doing math together unpleasant instead of fun. Many adults have difficulty conserving volume. If you ever chose the wrong container when putting away leftovers, you know how hard this can be.

MEASURING WEIGHT

◦ ◦ ◦ ◦ ◦ **To perform weight experiments** in a way that is meaningful to a young child, you need a pan balance. If you do not have one, you can create a scale from a wire hanger and the bottom and lid of a cardboard box. The lid will be turned upside down to create a second, open box. Use string to hang these from the sides of the hanger. A baggie tie in each corner of the hanger will prevent the strings from sliding along the base.

Find a place that the hanger can hang freely and the child can reach the boxes. If one side is heavier than the other (the lid is slightly larger but may be less deep), adjust this by taping paper clips or pennies to the underside of the lighter one until the pans are level. Do not count those as part of the weight of an object—they are part of the scale.

Look, my bear weighs the same as three tennis balls!

In order to weigh things, you will need a fixed unit of weight. Here again you can use pennies, paper clips, same-size Legos, or other uniform objects. Estimating weights, grouping in tens to count, and comparing weights will all be appropriate activities. At first the idea of weighing each object against a fixed type of counter is a very strange idea to children. They enjoy filling both sides of the scale with a variety of things and watching to see which side is heavier and what will make the pans balance. To help your child understand weight as a comparison to a fixed unit, you can make a written chart and record various objects and the number of paper clips (or whatever you are using for your unit) needed to balance each one. Label the headings of the two columns: "What we weighed" and "Weight measured in paper clips."

Once your child understands that, by this method, we can assign a weight measure to an object, you can move to more sophisticated work. After two toys have been weighed individually, questions like *How much do the mouse and rabbit weigh together?* lead to addition. To work on the idea of "How many more?" ask, *How much heavier is the rabbit than the mouse? How many more paper clips do we need to balance the rabbit?*

MEASURING TIME

● ● ● ● ● **Time can be measured** in handclaps. Set up a rhythm of evenly spaced claps. Take turns seeing how long you can stand on one leg, sing a note, not talk or laugh. Children can come up with ideas of things to time. You can record the numbers and then discuss questions like, *How many claps did you stand on one leg for? How many more claps did you stand on one leg than I did?* Remember that the point is to learn the use of numbers in measurement. If your child wants to "win" by standing or singing longer than you, let him. For you, this is not a competition but a chance to have fun with math together.

MEASUREMENT IN THE KITCHEN

● ● ● ● ● **Measurement is an integral part** of cooking and baking. It is easy to have fun with your children in the kitchen while getting them comfortable with common fractions and measurement. Children will see you use measuring tools, such as measuring cups and spoons, an oven temperature gauge, and a clock or timer, to make tasty things. They will see that you are careful about pouring the amount you want and about leveling the top of a measuring cup of dry ingredients. There can be a huge amount of math in cooking, but only if you discuss what you are doing.

> Comparing weights can demonstrate the meaning of both "adding on" and subtraction. These are discussed in chapter 7.

You might look at a recipe and decide to double it if you are making cookies to bring to a class or large party. *How many can fit on one cookie sheet?* Children love to count to find out how many there are. *Did we make more or fewer cookies than the recipe said?*

Children learn the meaning of the word "half" informally as things are shared. They may have some sense that it means they should get the same amount as the other person, or that it means part of something, but they do not relate this to the formal meaning of "1 divided by 2" that "½" represents. When you cook, your child can see the symbol "½" in the recipe and on the measuring cup or spoon. Help him understand the meaning by letting him play with water and measuring cups. *How many ½ cups will it take to fill 1 cup?* Did he figure this out before testing? Do the same with the ⅓ cup measurement, making sure that he sees the symbol "⅓." If your child knows the written numbers, see if he can guess how many ¼ cups will fill 1 cup.

Can you cook using only one measuring cup? You might try challenging yourself and talk out loud about what you are doing. For example, if one day you use only the ½ cup measure, what would you do to make 1 cup? What if the recipe calls for one fourth of a cup? How would you approximate that with the ½ cup? Challenge yourself and have your child be your helper: *Does that look like half?* You can enjoy being in the kitchen with your child, and he will practice numbers while making something good to eat.

Important ideas from chapter 4 for you to think about

▼▲▼▲

Estimate measurements and then check them to improve your own sense of size while showing that you don't always need to be precise.

Use measurement to increase your child's number sense, at whatever level is appropriate:
- counting
- two-digit place value
- fractions—seeing them used, although not yet fully comprehending
- decimals—hearing about them, but not yet learning anything formal
- multiplication
- estimation

There are a great variety of types of measurements commonly used at home:
- linear
- volume
- time
- weight
- area
- capacity
- temperature

▲▼▲▼

Let your child participate in as many measurement experiences as possible.

5

Playing with Shapes

Geometry

● ● ● ● ●

Geometry is a natural subject for play. Toddlers often play with shapes and take great pleasure from fitting a block to the correct hole. Concepts such as "above and below," "over and under," "in front of and behind," "next to" and later "to the right or left of" are all part of spatial thinking. When you use these terms with your child, you are helping her build a mathematical foundation.

When you do a giant jigsaw puzzle together, you use what artists call "positive and negative space," as well as match colors, lines, and patterns. Picture books pair the names

Playing with a shape-sorter is a favorite toddler activity.

of shapes with photos, drawings, and paintings of objects that have those shapes.

Many people who are uncomfortable with numbers or algebra find that geometry is a subject they enjoy. You may have taken a geometry course in high school. Usually those courses were taught without providing years of building a sense of shapes and their relationships, making geometry a mysterious subject. When you play with your child, you can prevent this problem by including enjoyable activities with shapes.

NAMING SHAPES

Young children learn to recognize and name circles, squares, triangles, rectangles, and diamonds. When creating and playing with shapes, make sure to use many different kinds of triangles to emphasize that it is the number of sides that determines the name.

> The word "triangle" literally means "three angles," but because most other shapes are named by the number of sides —quadrilateral, pentagon, hexagon —it is more consistent to use the number of sides to determine names.

These figures are all triangles even though they have different shapes and are placed in different positions.

Most children will not recognize a square when it is rotated into the "diamond" position.

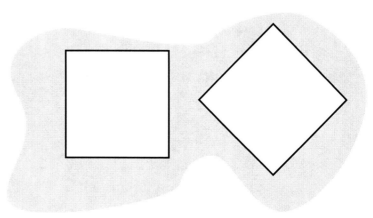

They are likely to argue that the figure has changed shape, even though it may be made of rigid material. This is normal, so be sure to avoid an argument. Let your child develop descriptive vocabulary of her own as you talk about shapes. In math, a four-sided figure with all sides of equal length is called a "rhombus" and the plural is "rhombi." This definition includes

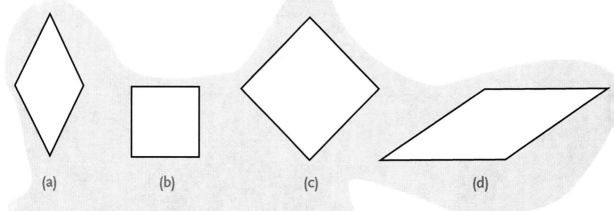

(a)   (b)   (c)   (d)

These are rhombi. Notice that (b) and (c) are both squares.

both squares and "diamonds." You can show how a square "turns into" a rhombus (diamond) and vice versa. Include rhombi (diamonds) that are not squares, and let your child turn them to see that they do not look like squares in any position, and leave it at that. Similarly, children have difficulty with the idea that a square is a special kind of rectangle. We usually try to use the most precise word we know, so we say "square" when we see one, and not "rectangle". Because of this, children have no way to know that a square also fits the definition of a rectangle: a four-sided figure with four right angles. Children want everything to be sharply distinguished and will resist this idea—that something can have two names at once. We won't expect them to accept it yet, but will prepare them for it by defining rectangles as four-sided shapes with all corners the same (instead of as a shape with two long and two short sides). Then it will be possible to notice that a square is a rectangle but limited to those with all sides of equal length. The ability to make these distinctions—"all Dalmatians are dogs, but not all dogs are Dalmatians"—will come with age.

VISUALIZING SHAPES

● ● ● ● ● **The following game** is one that young children love. The second version of it can help them to see the rhombus/square connection. Without your child seeing, take a common household item or toy and wrap it in a towel or, if available, a cloth bag with a drawstring. Choose something with a distinctive enough shape to be recognized through the fabric. Let your child feel the object through the cloth—not by putting hands inside the bag or towel. Can she guess what it is? Of course, let her hide something for you to guess. The act of creating a mental picture of the object and its shape through the sense of touch is excellent preparation for developing knowledge of shapes.

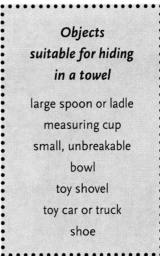

Objects suitable for hiding in a towel

large spoon or ladle

measuring cup

small, unbreakable bowl

toy shovel

toy car or truck

shoe

If you make a set of shapes cut out of thick cardboard, you can give her one behind her back. Let her feel it to identify it, without looking. Don't miss the looks of concentration and then pleasure and pride that she is likely to have as she examines and then solves this puzzle. Then have her give you a shape behind your back to figure out.

Common two-dimensional shapes and their definitions

polygon: a closed figure with straight sides

quadrilateral: a polygon with four sides

parallelogram: a quadrilateral with opposite sides parallel

kite: two pairs of adjacent congruent sides

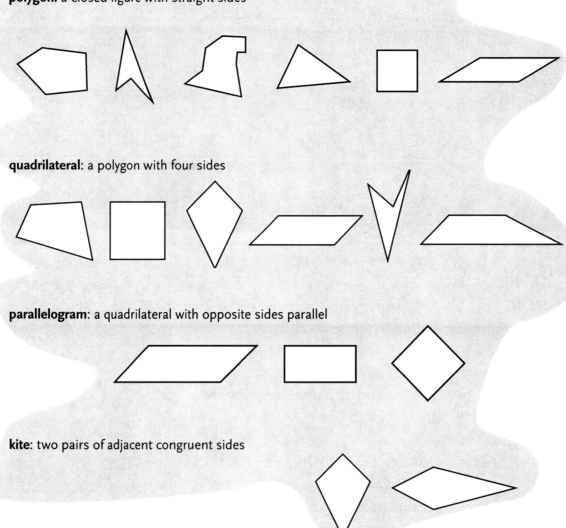

pentagon: a five-sided polygon

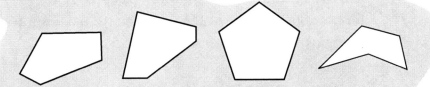

hexagon: a six-sided polygon

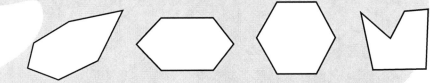

octagon: an eight-sided polygon

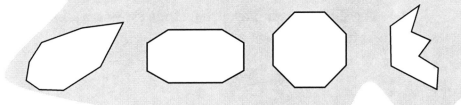

THREE-DIMENSIONAL SHAPES

• • • • • **Children absorb vocabulary** through repetition as they hear you use a word and see the object it refers to. This means that your correct use of terms is an important part of their learning, even though the results may not be immediate. Keep in mind some basic properties of shapes as you talk about them. Use different words for two-dimensional shapes and three-dimensional ones. Most of the blocks in the shape sorter toy are prisms. A prism is an object with two parallel, polygonal faces that are connected by faces that are parallelograms. Again, we won't expect the children to learn this word yet, but you can talk about the block that has two "sides" (in formal geometry these are called faces) that are stars, as opposed to saying that the block itself is a star.

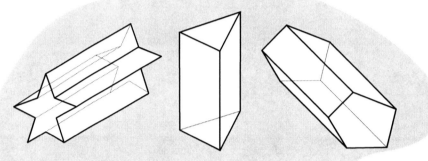

Prisms have a pair of parallel faces connected by parallelograms.

The shape sorter may also include cylinders—and perhaps an ellipsoidal cylinder.

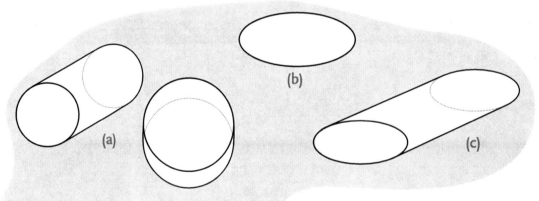

(a) two cylinders
(b) an ellipse (a two-dimensional shape)
(c) an ellipsoidal cylinder

Thinking about dimensions will also help you remember to refer to a sphere as a "ball," and not a "circle."

TALKING ABOUT ANGLES

● ● ● ● ● **When exploring shapes** with your child, identify them by the number of sides and the number of corners. Talk about lengths of sides—some figures have sides that are all the same length, some have sides of different lengths. Some have sides that are curved, while others have straight sides. You can observe some figures with very pointy corners, like the letter "V," some with corners like the upper case "L," (helpful with letter recognition) and others that are not very sharp at all.

> Discussion of perimeter, area, volume, and capacity began in chapter 4.

Types of angles:

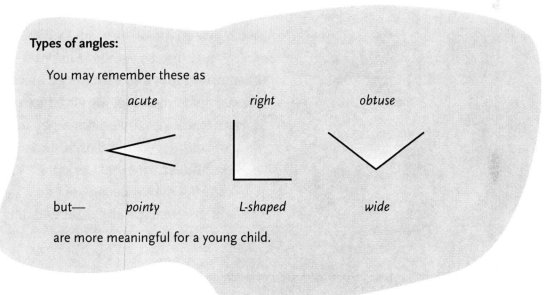

You may remember these as

acute   right   obtuse

but—   pointy   L-shaped   wide

are more meaningful for a young child.

The letters of the alphabet are a good source of shapes to observe and discuss. Some are closed figures, like the letter "D." These figures enclose a part of the paper. Some are open, like the letters "E" and "S," and some are combinations, like the letter "R."

THINKING ABOUT GEOMETRY WHILE PLAYING WITH TOYS

● ● ● ● ● **Playing with blocks** is an excellent way to become familiar with the properties of shapes in a tactile way. When you join in, you can add words to this activity. My children and I spent many enjoyable hours with a set of small, identical, rectangular-prism blocks. They used them for imaginative play to build doll-houses and animal corrals. We made walls and bridges and stood them up like dominoes and knocked them over. Careful placement meant that all the blocks would fall: the paths could be straight or curved, and the distance between the blocks could vary, but only by limited amounts. Sometimes the simplest toys allow for the greatest variety of games. Playing with blocks can lead to an understanding of volume, enclosed area, and perimeter, and that the same number of blocks can enclose different-shape and different-size areas.

Traditional school blocks come in "bricks," "longs," "cylinders," "wedges," "arches," and many other shapes.

If you have blocks of different shapes, count the number of faces on each block and name the shapes of those faces. With help, six-year-olds can make a guessing game in which each face of a block is traced on one sheet of paper, and another person is asked to figure out which block was used.

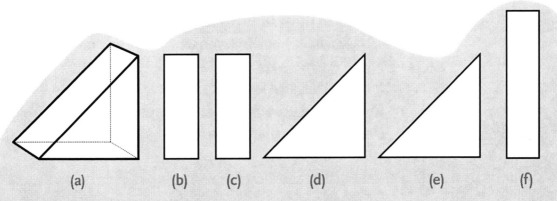

(a) This block is a triangular prism.
(b– f) These five shapes are the outlines of its five faces. Three of the faces are rectangles and two are triangles. You may be surprised by the length of face (f).

If you have traditional school blocks, there are "bricks" and "longs," the longs having twice the length of the bricks with the same height and width. If you use longs to measure the length of a rug or the width of a room, can your child guess how many will be needed to measure the same length with bricks? Does she realize that the answer will be a larger number? It is often surprising how young children comprehend this inverse relationship (smaller blocks mean a larger amount is needed to measure the same length). Well before they can add or multiply to come up with the exact number, they know that the answer will be bigger. This activity demonstrates multiplication before we expect children to learn it.

You and your child can make many simple puzzles for each other to solve. Using cardboard, cut several squares of the same size. Take one square and cut it into two pieces with a single straight cut. What shapes can you make with these two pieces by putting them together in different ways? Have your child make some puzzles for you. Can you put them together so that they form the square again? If she is not yet able to use scissors, have her show you where she wants the cut.

It's not always necessary to use a straight cut or to limit this to two pieces, but this is a simple way to begin. You can also start with shapes other than a square.

See pp. 167 and 169.

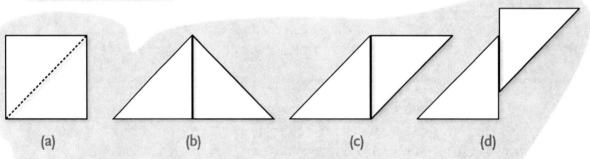

(a)   (b)   (c)   (d)

(a) A square cut diagonally. The two pieces were reassembled to form a:
    (b) triangle
    (c) parallelogram
    (d) hexagon

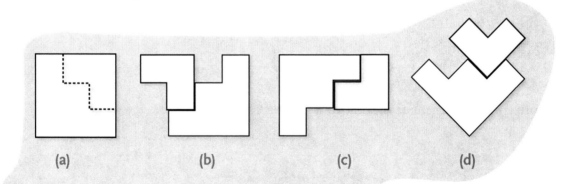

(a)   (b)   (c)   (d)

(a) This square was cut like steps. The two pieces were reassembled to look like, with some imagination:
    (b) a duck
    (c) a flag
    (d) a cat

You may be familiar with the ancient Chinese puzzle called a tangram. This is made from a square cut into seven pieces. It is usually difficult for young children to use all seven pieces to create the tangram figures. However, if you have a set and want to use it, buy or make pages that show the puzzle's solution. These contain the outline of the pieces. Just matching the shape and position of each piece is an appropriate challenge for young children.

Simpler four- and five-piece puzzles

A Web search on "5-piece tangram" yields many sources with different four- and five-piece puzzles.

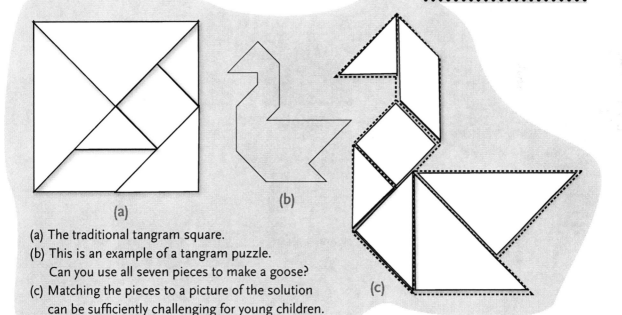

(a)

(b)

(c)

(a) The traditional tangram square.
(b) This is an example of a tangram puzzle. Can you use all seven pieces to make a goose?
(c) Matching the pieces to a picture of the solution can be sufficiently challenging for young children.

See pp. 171 to 175.

Three-dimensional puzzles can be made from clay or play dough. Make a cube or rectangular prism. Using a straight cut, slice it into two pieces. Can your child put the pieces together to make the original shape again? What other figures can be formed? What imaginative names can you give them?

Pattern blocks and area

Some of the pattern blocks (triangle, blue rhombus, trapezoid, and hexagon) have areas that are multiples of each other. They can later be used for understanding fractions. We'll talk about how to do that in volume 2.

Pattern blocks are another material that can provide years of pleasure. These are blocks that are all the same thickness, with yellow hexagons, blue rhombi, red trapezoids, green triangles, orange squares, and white narrow rhombi. All of these, except the trapezoids, have edges the same length.

Making designs, stacking and sorting the blocks help young children see the relationships between the

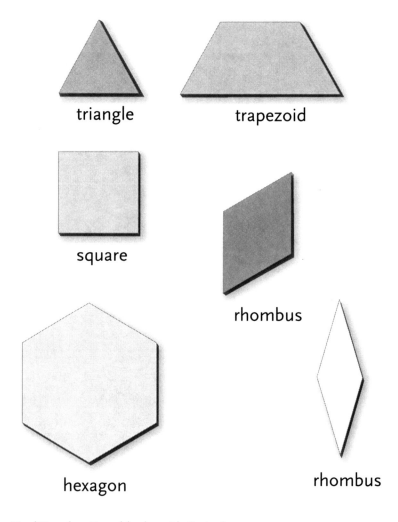

triangle　　　trapezoid

square

rhombus

hexagon　　　rhombus

Traditional pattern blocks with their shape names.

shapes. These activities prepare the way for learning about more complex mathematical relationships in years to come. You will find that blocks are relaxing and fun to use and a fine way to have play time with your child.

A design made with pattern blocks.

Important ideas from chapter 5 for you to think about

▽ ▲ ▼ ▲ ▽

Shapes are generally named by the number and types of sides or angles.

Discussion of shapes provides another opportunity to develop language.

Differentiate between two- and three-dimensional figures when working with your child.

Alongside your child, with free-form play, take shapes apart and reassemble them.

▲ ▽ ▲ ▽ ▲

Playing with toys that have built-in mathematical relationships (for example tangrams, pattern and building blocks) can help children learn math.

However, understanding will develop only if you talk about the relationships so your children become aware of them. Ongoing conversations are necessary.

6

Understanding Our Number System
Place Value

● ● ● ● ● ●

3 4 5

After a child learns to count it still takes many years to fully understand the place value number system that we use. Be patient. Humans spent thousands of years doing mathematics before inventing a place value system—one in which the placement of the digits determines the value it represents. For example, in the number 345, the 3 represents three hundreds, the 4 represents four tens while the 5 is just five ones. Although the 3 has the smallest value of the digits when it is used alone, in this number it represents the largest amount of all the digits because of its position. If you have used Roman numerals, you know that although the position of the symbols plays a role in their value, it is not a place value system: each letter represents the same amount, no matter where it is placed.

Scientific notation

Scientific notation is a way of writing numbers that eliminates counting out the place value of the columns in large and small numbers. For example, 23,000,000,000,000 written this way requires us to count along the sections to figure out that this number is 23 trillion. In scientific notation, this number would be written 2.3×10^{13}. With an understanding of place value we can quickly compare and make sense of extremely large and small numbers.

Understanding our number system is the basis for a large part of the math done throughout elementary school. When a child writes "1003" to mean "one hundred three," it is evident that he does not understand the place value system. It is less obvious when a child makes this very common error:

$$
\begin{array}{r}
38 \\
+\ 47 \\
\hline
715
\end{array}
$$

A COMMON ERROR IN ADDITION

This demonstrates that an understanding of place value is missing, and that what is needed is not just memorization of the rules for addition.

Children often have trouble learning arithmetic with place value, yet place value is also what makes arithmetic simple once we do understand it. Place-value learning will continue to develop until about eighth grade when students learn scientific notation. Once they are able to use scientific notation, they have a thorough understanding of place value. This ability will affect the child's work in mathematics, science, social studies, and economics.

NAMING NUMBERS OVER TEN

● ● ● ● ● **Let's begin** by looking at how young children learn the place value system. Children become familiar with two-digit numbers by seeing them and hearing them. They are learning to say the numbers in the proper order and may see the written pattern that accompanies this. As was mentioned in chapter 1, most of our number names are said in the order in which we read them, from left to right as in 345, which is "three hundred forty-five."

There are a few exceptions: for 13 through 19 we say the ones place first and then the tens place, as in "thirteen" (meaning "three" and "ten"). We read from left to right, but for the numbers 13 through 19 we say the place values in reverse order of the written number. This is difficult for young children to master; they are likely to write "31" when they mean "13." It is helpful if you recognize that this difference in spoken and written numbers causes confusion. Make sure that your child both sees and hears two-digit numbers at the same time. This can occur in elevators, on roads with speed limits and route-number signs, and by saying numbers that he sees you write.

When your child regularly counts amounts over 20 correctly and can count aloud to 100 with few errors, you can begin activities that will help him to understand the place value system. Extend your set of number cards to 100 (see chapter 1). Let your child help to create these. *How many cards have two-digit numbers that begin with the digit 2? How many two-*

digit numbers begin with the digit 3? Your child might want to count them to find out or to check. Give your child a set of number cards to put in order. You might begin with 1–40 and increase by tens.

Estimating the length of the number line you make

While placing number cards in order, you might ask, *How long do you think the line will be when the cards are placed next to each other on the floor?* Through practice, children become better at making estimates, and this is a natural place to make one. However, it is important to realize that if your child is afraid of being wrong, estimating can be an upsetting experience. An estimate is not usually the exact answer. If you find that your child is anxious about estimating, don't force him to do so. You should make your estimate out loud and share the thought process by which you chose your number. Then he will see that you are comfortable about not having the precise answer. You might also express your sense of how well you estimated: *That was a pretty close guess. I saw that almost five number cards fit in one floor tile, so I had a good idea of how many floor tiles would be covered* or, *That estimate was very far off. The cards go farther than I thought.*

MAKING GROUPS OF TENS AND ONES

●　●　●　●　● **Also practice counting by tens.** At first children learn this as a chant, *10, 20, 30, . . .* and although they know it's related to counting, they do not connect the words with the appropriate amounts. We know this when we see a child counting single items and saying, *10, 20, 30, . . .* This is normal. The chant is important because children must learn this sequence in order. Learning it helps them count by ones as well. To see whether your child's counting by tens has meaning, take objects that you have grouped in tens in front of him, such as 2 or 3 stacks of ten pennies each, and ask him to count them by tens.

Does he take one object at a time while he says, *10, 20, 30 . . .* or does he take a stack of ten when he says *ten*? When he takes a group of ten pennies and says *ten*, you know that he understands the words as amounts, not as some magical thing that people say as they move objects.

> 10,20,30, 31,**32!**

> Great! She used to count 10,20,30,40,50. Now she knows it's 32!

Counting by ones remains an important part of this process. A child needs to know that 85 comes long after 58 in the counting sequence. Objects you might count are: silverware, buttons in a button collection, blocks or any other toy that has many pieces, pennies, and paper clips. Make sure that you sometimes have 100 objects. Invite your child to estimate the number of pieces before beginning the count. Then make one yourself. After he counts them, both of you put them in groups of ten, because now the goal of counting is to build understanding of place value. The idea is to have him connect "58" with "5 groups of 10 and 8 more."

With enough experience, children switch from saying a rote chant of numbers to counting the number of objects.

Buttons are excellent for counting. Children enjoy the varied colors, textures, and shapes. If you have a button collection, let your child count them or find some small objects to count. Invite him to write the number on a piece of paper if he has shown interest in doing so, or write it yourself. Because he is also learning to read, include the word for what you have counted, such as "58 buttons."

I have found the following place-value activities very useful when working with children in schools. Little children like to play school, so long as they are the teacher. Make sure that as you introduce these activities, you take turns with his ideas. Realize that if he is resistant, it means that he feels uncomfortable and that you will need to wait before trying these again. Be careful to use a positive tone when doing math with your child. With that advice, the next activity you might introduce is to ask, *If we make stacks with ten same-size Legos in each stack, how many stacks do you think there will be?* Assuming that you have already counted 58 blocks, at first your child's answer may be 58, or any seemingly random number. Do not be disturbed—that is why you are doing this activity. When he knows immediately that 58 means "5 groups of ten and 8 left over," you will move on to the next level.

You can both work to place objects in groups of ten. Besides the blocks that can be stacked in towers of ten, empty egg cartons can be used to hold buttons, paper clips, pennies, and other small objects. Cups or bowls can be used for larger ones. Circles of string can accommodate any size and can be corrals for animals or parking lots for cars

Toy cars can be grouped in tens and ones: 2 groups of ten each and 3 extra cars outside makes 23 cars.

If you use an egg carton, cut two cups off an end so that when filled, the carton will contain 100 objects, ten in each cup. You will not be working on hundreds yet, but this will provide some experience with one hundred. Tell your child why you are cutting the cartons. Have him check that there are ten cups for holding objects. Count ten objects into each cup. Then count by tens to show this method of counting. Invite him to count the number of items. Seeing that there are 100 of something can be quite exciting. Later you will use the egg carton to make obvious the relationship of 5 tens and 8 ones to 58.

Another way to emphasize the use of ten in our number system is to make hundreds, tens, and ones. You can use full boxes of paper clips to represent "hundreds," chains of ten paper clips for your "tens," and loose paper clips as "ones." You can also use graph paper to create "hundreds" (10 × 10 squares), "tens" (10 × 1 strips), and "ones" (1 × 1 small squares). Use paper that has at least ½-inch boxes, so that the pieces are easy to handle.

An egg carton can be cut to have ten cups. When each cup is filled with ten pennies, paper clips, or beads, the carton contains 100 objects.

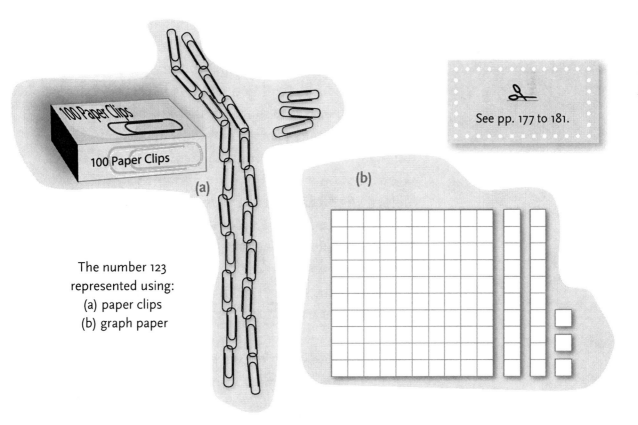

See pp. 177 to 181.

The number 123 represented using:
(a) paper clips
(b) graph paper

Legos put in stacks of ten can measure the length of a stuffed toy.

A stacking toy such as Lego is good for this purpose, too. A material that embodies our number system even more closely is Digi-Blocks, which pack into boxes of tens, hundreds and thousands. All of these materials have the advantage that your child can immediately recognize that a group of ten is equivalent to ten loose ones, and it is natural to switch between thinking of them as "one ten" and as "ten ones" by taking them apart and putting them back together. This is vital. Young children prefer things that are simple: stories with heroes and villains, rather than more complex characters; they resist the idea that a square is both a rectangle and a square. But in order to use our number system effectively, it is necessary to be flexible, and to see a number many different ways. Using one of these materials, make groups of ten with your child. Compare them to see that they are all the same size. Some toys come in a variety of colors, so you can make a blue stack and a red stack, etc. When the stacks are combined, each set of ten will stand out from the others. If your stacking toy is one color, use masking tape or some other easy-to-remove marker and put it on the topmost piece to mark the tenth item.

In chapters 4 and 9 there are activities that help develop a child's understanding of place value through measurement.

How many blocks did we stack? If your child doesn't count by tens, do so with him after he has made his count. Throughout the next few chapters I will refer to these stacks, chains, blocks, graph-paper strips, and paper clips that are arranged to show ones, tens, and hundreds, as "base-ten materials." You will use whichever of these you prefer or have handy.

ADDING TENS

Once your child sees the relationship between tens and ones, he is ready for more challenging questions. Give him about 33 objects to count. Ask, *How many will you have if I give you ten more?* If he does not know, give him the ten objects, in a stack or group, and ask him to find out how many there are. If he does know, give the objects and then ask the same question, *How many will you have if I give you ten more?* Continue to ask him to add ten more. If he needs to count to find the answer, let him do so. If he gets the answer without counting audibly, ask, *How did you get that answer?*

> ### How did you get that answer?
>
> Ask this question whether the answer is right or wrong. This is extremely important in all of your work with your child. Because you are helping him develop mathematical thinking, it is the thought process that you need to know as well as the answer.

DECODING OUR NUMBER SYSTEM

Here is an example of the importance of knowing how your child found an answer. A child who has begun to understand the place value system, who knows immediately that 10 more than 33 is 43, should be given work that is different from what you give a child who has to count 10 up from 33 to get 43. Both children have the correct answer. However, the child who knows that adding one to the tens place is the same as adding ten separate ones has broken the code of our number system, while the child who counts ten more has not yet done so. Children who know the code should next be asked to add and subtract multiples of 10 from two-digit numbers. For example, ask, *How many will there be if we add 20 to the 43? If we take away 30, how many will we have then?* Those who haven't yet caught on need to continue to work on the place-value activities discussed above. You must know how your child is thinking in order to find the appropriate next question. And don't forget to give your child a turn at asking you questions about how many there are.

A child might know that 10 more than 33 is 43, and 10 more is 53, but then say that 10 more is 73. Some children will have understood the pattern of change before attaining a solid memory of the order of the multiples of ten and the ability to work carefully. It is normal to have many parts of learning occur simultaneously. This is why counting, by both ones and tens, continues to be an important part of your work together. Similarly, many children who know how to count fairly well will make errors when counting large numbers of objects. This is normal at this stage. Decide if it is appropriate to supply the correct number, to have your child check the count, or to ignore it. If he didn't get it right, make sure he counts this amount soon again. Then you will find out if it is a repeated mistake, requiring correction, or a careless error that he fixes himself with practice.

When children are learning about two-digit and larger numbers, I tell them that our number system is a "secret code." One must be in on the secret of the meanings of the place values in order to know what the numbers represent. 32 does not mean 3, then 2, or 3 + 2. Only those who know the code—that the 3 in 32 stands for 3 tens—can make sense of our numbers. This imagery appeals to children, especially those in the neighborhood of six to seven years old, and accurately describes the difficult system they are trying to learn.

PLACE VALUE WITH MEASUREMENT

● ● ● ● ● **Length measurement** can be used to increase the understanding of place value. A way to have your child discover the relationship of tens, ones, and the way we name and write numbers is to ask, *What can you find that is as long as three ten-stacks of Legos (or three 10 × 1 paper strips)?* Have your child look around and find an object with length approximately the same as three stacks (or three paper strips). Next he should use the stacks or paper strips and some loose ones to get a more exact measurement of the object and write the measurement.

Remember to record the item measured as well as the length. The final question, and the most significant for finding out about his understanding of place value is to ask, *If we count all the little pieces, in the stacks and the extra ones, how many will there be?*

You can prepare a page for recording the lengths of several objects:

What I Measured	Number of ten-stacks (or strips)	Number of extra ones	Total number of blocks (or clips or squares)
Snake	4	3	43

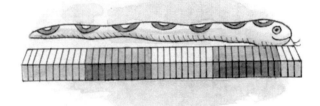

To find out your child's understanding of place value, notice whether he knows immediately that, for example, 3 ten-stacks and 2 ones is 32 blocks in all, or whether he needs to count all the pieces to find out. If your child knows the answer immediately, go on to more challenging work. If he does not yet see the relationship, have him measure several objects that are about the length of 5 ten-stacks. If he does not want to do all the counting, it will be an incentive to find a short cut. Encourage him to look for one. It is a real treat to see your child make the discovery that he doesn't need to count all the pieces. The pleasure that accompanies "fooling you," getting the answer without work and realizing that he has uncovered a major idea of our number system, helps children to feel their power as mathematical thinkers. For this reason it is important that you not hurry your child into this realization or take it away from him by pointing out the relationship yourself. Remember that we are trying to build his mathematical thinking and confidence in his ability to solve problems. These goals are much greater than just having him say the correct answer!

Area measurement can also be used to increase understanding of place value. Area is measured in squares. Formal area measurement is given in square feet, inches, and meters. As we did with linear measurement, begin with something less abstract. You can use squares of colored paper to find the area of a desktop, book cover, rug, or other rectangular shape. Many message pads are square and, with the aid of a binder clip, can return to that use when you are done.

When your child is measuring, have him place the squares in groups of ten and count them by tens. Because conservation of area is much more difficult than conservation of linear measurement, your child might think that rearranged squares have an area different from the original shape you set out to measure. This, too, is normal, and understanding will come with experience.

Let your children watch when you are engaged in math activities. If you cut squares from larger paper, make sure that your child sees how you create them.

Conservation of number, length, area, and volume are the knowledge that the total amount stays the same, even if the location or shape have changed. This idea is discussed in chapter 1.

Important ideas from chapter 6 for you to think about

▽ ▲ ▽ ▲ ▽ ▲

Place value understanding is basic to most elementary school math.

Children must become able to think of numbers in more than one way; for example ten is "1 ten," "10 ones," "8 + 2," "two fives," all at the same time.

Help your child to see the patterns in our number system:

- count groups of about 100 items by ones
- count by tens
- group objects by tens to count them
- write the numbers

Listen to see if your child can:

- count one-to-one for more than twenty objects
- say the numbers in order between 20 and 30, between 30 and 40, etc., when you supply the multiple of 10
- count by tens
- group objects by tens to find out how many there are

▲ ▽ ▲ ▽ ▲ ▽

Ask your children how they got their answers, whether they are right or wrong. Use the information to decide the next question to ask.

7

Addition

Beginning to Add (and Subtract)

●●●●●●●

There are many aspects of learning addition and subtraction besides the rules that you memorized in school to get the correct answer. First, a child must understand the meaning of adding: putting two groups together and finding out how many there are in the combined set. This idea is separate from being able to find the answer. The symbol "+," which your child will eventually learn, indicates that two groups are being combined. But before that symbol is introduced, it is important to help your child learn addition orally (or "mentally," as doing non-written math is often described). Because we use words like "and" and "add" in daily life to mean the same thing that they mean in math, the idea of addition is usually grasped quickly and naturally. It takes longer to find efficient ways to find the sum, but that is a separate project. A good way to begin is by taking numbers apart and putting them back together.

TAKING NUMBERS APART

● ● ● ● ● **Separating a quantity into two groups** is an important number activity. It is an indirect part of counting and leads to understanding addition and subtraction. One aspect of understanding counting is realizing that each number is one more than the one before. The number two is one more than one. Two can be formed from two separate ones. Three is one more than two. It can be taken apart to make a group of size two and another of size one.

FIND OUT WHAT SIZE NUMBER YOUR CHILD CAN SEPARATE INTO TWO GROUPS IN HER HEAD.

● ● ● ● ● ● Play **"Break the Stack Behind Your Back"** using Lego bricks that are all the same size, or some other stacking toy. Make a stack of a few blocks and have your child count them. Place the stack behind your back, break it into two shorter stacks and bring one stack forward for your child to see. Then ask, *How many blocks are behind my back?*

If you do not have a stacking toy or if you want to vary the game, play "How Many Pennies?" Take some pennies and count them with your child. Make sure that you both know how many there are. Put some of the pennies in the closed fist of one hand and some in the

Children enjoy the game "Break the Stack Behind Your Back."

other. Do not let her see how many are in each hand. Have her choose a hand and show her the pennies in that hand. Ask, *How many pennies do you think are in the other hand?*

If she is unable to make a guess or find the answer, invite her to take the same number of blocks or pennies that you started with and see if she can use them to figure out how many are behind your back or in your closed hand. Does she remember how many you started with? Make sure to begin the next round with a smaller total until you have found the number at which she is able to figure out the answer. After she responds, ask, *How did you get the answer?* Be careful not to say whether or not the answer is correct! Just ask and listen. Ask, *Would you like to check by seeing the stack (or what is in the other hand)?* Then let her take a turn with the same total number of blocks or pennies. If the pennies don't fit in her hand, they can be placed under and on the base of an upside-down cup or bowl.

There were five pennies in all. How many pennies can you see? How many are hidden under the cup?

Continue to play this, adjusting the total number up or down so that she is working to find the answer, but is able to do so.

Use what you learned to help your child

Does your child "just know" the answer, right away in her head? Is she able to figure it out using her fingers or by saying the numbers in counting order? Can she use reasoning like this: *You have five pennies. There are two in this hand that I see. I know 2 + 2 = 4, so you must have three because 2 + 3 = 5.* Does she need to be given her own set of pennies to figure out the answer?

> A little math done often is best. Sometimes you may forget to do math for a while, and then are surprised when your child doesn't know something that you thought she had learned. At that point, don't insist on doing math for a long session. Remember to recognize the level of your child's enjoyment as well as level of math.

(The same total amount of pennies should be beside her so she can use them if she needs to.) Is your child at a complete loss to find a way to answer this question? Don't worry. It only means that she requires much more counting of small amounts. Demonstrate using a group of three objects: hide two and show one; then hide one and show two; hide three and show none; hide none and show three. If necessary, count the pennies together. If your child does have a means of finding the answer, play the game gradually using higher or lower numbers until you find the number that your child does not "just know" in her head. Stay with that amount until she knows the pairs "in her head." Then increase the total by one.

Your goal is to have your child be able to separate the numbers to twenty so quickly in her head that she can't explain how she did it. Today you may be playing the game with three pennies and practicing counting to five because you have noticed that that is enough work for now. A little bit of counting and a few games played more often are best. Let her make the rules for a game and play that as well as your version.

LEARNING TO ADD

Parents often become frustrated watching a child who, when adding 4 + 3, first counts that there are four in one group, three in another, joins the groups together, and then begins to count from one again. You want your child to progress to "counting on." This means remembering the count of 4 and being able to count onwards by saying, *5, 6, 7* as the additional three objects are counted (or beginning with 3 and counting on 4 more, *4, 5, 6, 7*; knowing to start with the larger number is a further refinement that you will point out when appropriate). Remembering that she already counted four relates to her ability to conserve numbers. Does she believe that there are still four objects in that group, even when the group has been moved to join the other? A child who continues to count from one after repeated exposures to "counting on" may not yet conserve numbers. If your child does not yet conserve numbers, spend time with those activities before you work on addition.

"Conservation of number" is explained in chapter 1.

If conservation is not the issue, provide many experiences with the same small numbers, using different materials and contexts. A teacher I know has found a method that helps his unsure students move towards counting on. He has them bump their fists to their foreheads as they say *four* and then count on. This signal to themselves that they already have the four in their heads adds the confidence some need. Demonstrate counting on by adding and counting aloud.

Once children understand the meaning of adding and can accurately count on, we want them to move to more sophisticated methods of performing addition. These rely on memorization and understanding number relationships. The simplest additive relationship is "one more." You can ask your child questions that involve adding one more. You can do this both concretely, with objects, and abstractly:

I know 4 . . . and 3 more makes 5, 6, 7!

Here are some marbles. How many do you have?
Here's one more. How many do you have now?
How did you get your answer?

If I have four marbles in my pocket, and then you
give me one more, how many will I have?

We want children to reach the point of knowing automatically that "one more" means the same as "the next counting number." Similar questions for "one less" should also be asked: *I have five marbles. If I give you one, how many will I have left?*

This is a good place to comment on counting on one's fingers. Many of us were told that it is bad to do so. Children (and adults) often feel the need to hide the fact that they use their fingers. For a young child, being able to answer simple addition questions by counting on fingers represents a first level of abstraction. The child already understands that the answer will be the same, whether she counts marbles, pennies, or fingers. The rules for the numbers apply, no matter what object they are attached to. This is a very important realization for a child and should not be treated as doing something wrong. Eventually, however, it is vital that number facts be committed to memory. If a child continues to count on fingers, it is important to develop the ability to use related number facts as a means to find answers and to practice sums repeatedly so that they become known from memory.

Most children naturally memorize a few basic facts, particularly $2 + 2$ and $5 + 5$. You might assist in this process by asking these questions often. Once a child knows that $2 + 2 = 4$, we want her to use that to figure out that $2 + 3 = 5$. Because three is one more than two, we know that the sum is one more than four. This complex thinking is one example of what is meant by "related number facts." Most children need large amounts of exposure to addition and counting in order to be able to build answers from memorized fact, although some children catch on extremely quickly.

Memorization of basic arithmetic facts is a necessary part of the process of learning addition and subtraction. The "basic facts" refer to sums and differences of the numbers up to 10 and eventually up to 20. Once these are known and the place value system understood, addition of any numbers below 100 is nearly instantaneous. The game "Break the Stack Behind Your Back" (see page 92) is one way to help your child learn small sums. When we answer a question such as *There were five Legos in the hidden stack and now I've broken off two and shown them to you; how many are still behind my back?* it's hard to say if we find the answer by adding, subtracting, or *just knowing it in our heads*, as the children who have memorized a sum say. We so thoroughly know the parts of five that we do not consciously add or subtract. We automatically see five as 0 + 5, 1 + 4, 2 + 3, 3 + 2, 4 + 1, and 5 + 0. We do not need to make any conscious effort to recognize each of these pairs as "5." The entire set of related number facts is immediately known to us. In school such a set of facts is sometimes referred to as a "fact family."

$$2 + 3 = 5 \quad 3 + 2 = 5 \quad 5 = 2 + 3 \quad 5 = 3 + 2$$

$$5 - 3 = 2 \quad 5 - 2 = 3 \quad 2 = 5 - 3 \quad 3 = 5 - 2$$

The "fact family" for 2, 3, and 5 has eight facts. I've included all eight facts because when you move to writing equations, it is important for children to learn that the symbol "=" means that the same amount is on both sides. It does not mean "the answer."

Children need frequent practice in order to know these with certainty. It is important to create many situations in which children are combining groups or separating them and learning these relationships.

AN AMAZING CARD TRICK THAT HELPS CHILDREN MEMORIZE THE SUMS TO 10

● ● ● ● ●   **This card trick is truly splendid.** Teaching it to children is tremendous fun. I teach it in classes and love watching the spellbound faces and the joy as they catch on. When children know the sums of some of the small numbers, they can memorize the sums for 10 quite easily through this card trick. They do not experience this as the work of memorizing the sums for ten because they are focused on being successful at impressing others with magic. I learned this from my father when I was a child.

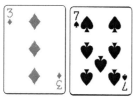

Use a standard deck of cards. The magician will mix the cards and invite someone to **remove one card from the deck and hide it**, promising to figure out the face value of the selected card, but not the suit.

The magician places the cards on the table, one at a time, face up. Whenever two cards are in view whose sum is 10, they are covered by the next two cards that leave the magician's hands. A number "10" card is also covered whenever it appears.

The picture cards, Jack, Queen and King, will be treated as if those three combined add to 10. **Whenever a complete set of Jack, Queen and**

King are face-up, all three will be covered by the next three cards. (Alternatively, the picture cards can be removed from the deck before starting the trick.)

An ace counts as the number 1 in this game, so it will partner with 9. Except for the Jack-Queen-King combination and the "10" alone, we will only use pairs that make 10.

When all the cards have been put into piles—by covering cards or by beginning a new pile if there are no ways to make ten—the piles are collected according to the same rules: a pile with a "10" on the top is picked up alone, two piles with cards on top that add to 10 are picked up together, and a combination of piles with Jack, Queen and King on the top are picked up together. The magician must work carefully to keep the piles neat so that it is clear what number is on top.

At the end, the magician is in one of the following situations:

1. There is a single pile left with any of the numbers "1" through "9" on top.
2. There are two piles with different picture cards showing.
3. There are no piles left.

If you have a single pile left with, for example, a "7" card on top, the missing card must be a "3", 7's partner to make 10. Similarly, if you have two picture cards left, for example a Jack and a King, the missing card must be a Queen. It's a little more difficult to figure out the missing card when you have no cards left on the table. It is a "10"—the only type of card that alone makes 10.

The Great Card Trick—A Sample

The Mystery Card

Magician says, *Pick a card, any card, and don't let me see it. I will figure out the number on your card, but not the suit.*

Card is taken by second person and hidden (e.g., in back pocket).

Magician holds the remaining deck face down.

Magician deals out cards one at a time, face up on the table. (Magician is looking for 10 —as a pair adding up to 10, as a "10" card, or by pretending that Jack + Queen + King = 10)

The first card was not a "10," so Magician starts a new pile of cards. No 10 yet, so Magician starts a third card pile.

---

2 + 8 = 10 so the next two cards dealt will . . .

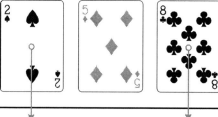

. . . cover the cards with the 2 and the 8 on them. Magician places the new cards face up on these piles. Now there are two "5"s!

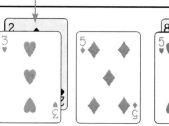

5 + 5 = 10 so Magician uses the next two cards to cover these.

It may be time to neaten the piles. Now there's nothing that makes 10 . . .

. . . so Magician starts a new pile. Still nothing that makes 10, so . . .

. . . Magician starts yet another pile.

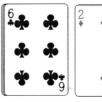

Ace counts as 1, but even though 6 + 3 + 1 = 10, we only use pairs of numbers that add to 10 (with two exceptions: "10" cards covered alone, and pretending that Jack + Queen + King = 10), so still no 10s.

Magician must start another pile. Magician wishes s/he didn't have to make so many piles. Magician starts it in a new row to make it easier to reach. It's another Jack, so it's time for yet another pile.

The next card is a "10" card. A "10" card alone counts as 10 . . .

. . . , so Magician covers the "10" with the next card. Now there are three picture cards, but not one each of Jack, Queen and King, so Magician must again start a new pile.

Now there are a "6" and a "4", so Magician will cover them . . .

. . . and make sure the piles are neat. There are now two more moves for Magician.

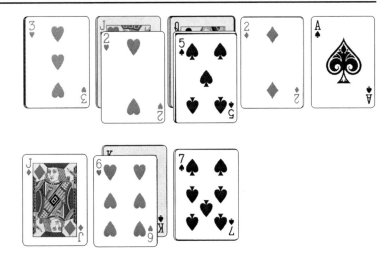

Magician uses the next three cards to cover one each of Jack, Queen and King. It doesn't matter which Jack is covered.

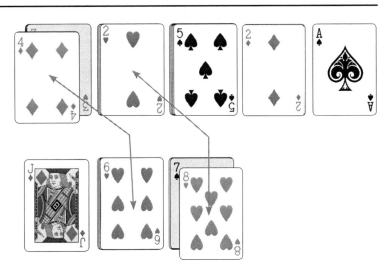

Next, Magician covers the "3" and the "7". Magician neatens the piles and sees that there are more pairs that add to 10 and so will cover the "6" and "4" and the "8" and "2" . . .

. . . Magician continues in this manner until all fifty-one cards are placed on the table. Some piles might have just one card, others will have many. Magician has just placed the last card on the table and has these piles:

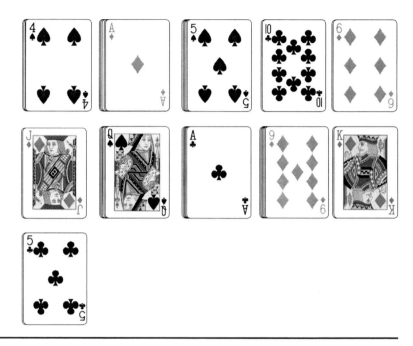

Once all the cards have been placed on the table, Magician picks up the piles using the same rules:

    If a "10" is on top, that pile is picked up alone.

    Two piles whose top cards add to 10 are picked up as a pair.

    Piles topped by Jack, Queen and King, (one of each) are picked up as a group.

Magician picks up the pile with "10" on top.

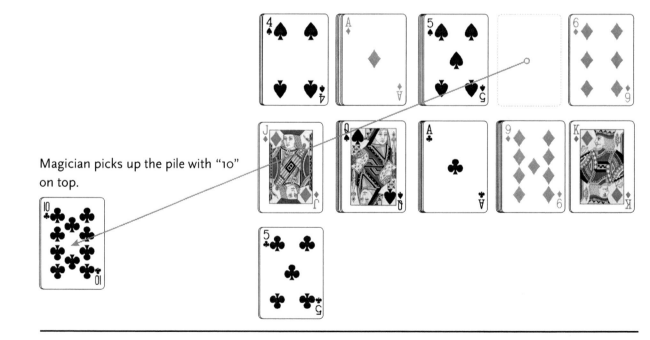

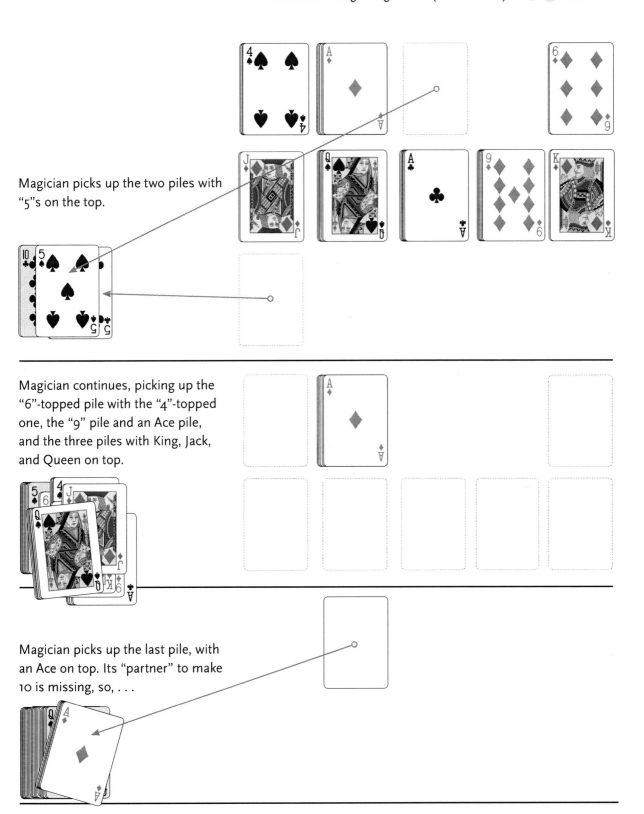

Magician picks up the two piles with "5"s on the top.

Magician continues, picking up the "6"-topped pile with the "4"-topped one, the "9" pile and an Ace pile, and the three piles with King, Jack, and Queen on top.

Magician picks up the last pile, with an Ace on top. Its "partner" to make 10 is missing, so, . . .

By my magic powers I figured out that your card is a "9"!

(Note: Remember, if the mystery card had been a face card, there would have been two piles remaining, each with a different kind of face card on top, and the mystery card would have been of the third kind; if the mystery card had been a "10", there would have been no piles remaining.)

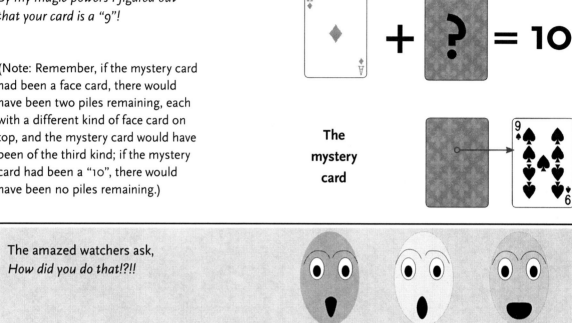

The mystery card

The amazed watchers ask, *How did you do that!?!!*

You will need to take a deck of cards and try this before you teach it to your child. Just remove a card and keep it face-down to see if you've done it right. This trick is very impressive to children who are just learning their sums, but equally so to much older people, who at first think that you are going to put all the aces together, then all the twos, and so on, which wouldn't be much of a trick. When they see you creating piles that seem arbitrary, they are quite mystified. Do not mention that you are using tens—otherwise you give it away.

It is very important that you not try to teach this trick before your child is ready for it. Otherwise it will be frustrating for her, causing bad associations, and when it becomes appropriate for her to learn it, she won't be interested. A child is ready to learn this trick when she is able to "add on" with numbers of this size. A child who counts from one for each sum is not ready. Children usually memorize 5 + 5 and 9 + 1 first, so this combination is a fine sign that the remaining sums can be learned with this trick.

QUESTIONS THAT YOU MIGHT NOT THINK OF AS ADDITION THAT INVOLVE JOINING TWO GROUPS

● ● ● ● ● **Addition can be viewed** as a process that joins two or more groups together. Many questions sound like addition but might be solved using subtraction instead of adding. The simplest type of question contains a situation in which the amount in each group is known and we want to find the total:

> *Cesar won eight prize tickets at the school fair. His big sister gave him three that she had won. How many tickets did Cesar have then?*

Here we know the sizes of the two groups to be joined. This is what we were taught to think of as an addition question in school. It is the easiest type for children to solve.

Here is a different arithmetic question. Even more than the answer to the question, I want you to be aware of how you find the answer.

> *Cesar won seven prize tickets playing games at the school fair. He wants a stuffed bear for which he needs twelve prize tickets. How many more tickets does he need to get the bear?*

Did you remember to observe how you got your answer? What did you notice? When I give an exercise like this to a group of adults, at least half find that they have solved it by using addition. They respond, *I know that 7 + 5 = 12, so he needs 5 more.* Some people use subtraction. *I know that 12 − 7 = 5.* I never had anyone report that they thought, *I borrowed a ten, changed it to ones, and then subtracted seven from those ones.*

A question of "how many more?" does not necessarily have to be answered using subtraction. However, when we were in school, we were told that a question about "more" is always a subtraction exercise. When I ask people to notice how they find the answers to such questions, they are often very surprised to realize that they don't use subtraction. When the numbers are large and far apart, subtraction often becomes the most efficient way to find the answer, but this depends on the numbers. Try to notice how you perform simple calculations in daily life. Perhaps your method isn't the one you were taught in school—but that doesn't matter—it's still real math!

It is very important for you to realize that there are many correct ways to do math. A child who does it a different way from the one you had in mind isn't necessarily wrong. Listen to your child's reasoning and see if it makes sense. If the answer is wrong, is it because the idea is wrong or because it was carried out wrong? Did you check that your child was working on the same question you thought she was?

In the second example on the previous page, we know the number of tickets that Cesar has when the situation begins. There is a second group consisting of the amount needed to reach his goal. These two groups will be joined together to make a total of 12. We can picture this as a joining operation. He plans to *add* more tickets to his collection until he can get the bear. It is quite challenging to answer a question in which the first addend (number to be added) and the total are given.

A third type of question begins with an unknown amount. This is the most difficult.

> *Cesar won a lot of tickets playing games at the school fair. He put them all in his pocket. At the end of the afternoon his big sister came over and said that he could have three of her tickets. Cesar thanked her and decided to see how many tickets he had all together. There were fifteen tickets. How many tickets did Cesar win at the fair?*

While it is likely that you found the answer by thinking $15 - 3 = 12$, the story contains another situation in which two groups have been joined together—Cesar's winnings and the gift from his sister.

I have detailed these types of joining questions to help you realize why children have a hard time knowing when to add and when to subtract. A situation that involves joining two groups together might be easier to solve with subtraction, as in the third example above. If the numbers were different—for example, if his sister gave him 379 tickets and at the end of the day he counted up a total of 435, using subtraction might be a much easier way to answer the question. But with small numbers, there is no need to force the use of subtraction if children have a more efficient way of finding the answer. We need to help children understand the interplay of addition and subtraction rather than order them to use one method in a given situation. In addition to the Lego or penny game, take turns making up story questions about objects you and your child are handling. Create a variety of question types. Give your child the time and space necessary to find ways to get the answer. Ask your child how she got her answer, whether or not the answer is correct. Share your own method with your child after she has told you or demonstrated hers.

Most of the mathematics learned in elementary school is applicable to simple activities and tangible objects. Many parents and teachers move too quickly, treating math as only an abstract subject. The adults seem afraid that children will not make the transition from the concrete to the abstract if they are allowed to thoroughly understand the concrete first. Some children find abstract methods of math enjoyable and easy to understand, but most children need many opportunities to use real objects. Pose questions that can be answered using those objects. When appropriate, show your child the abstract mathematical way to record the work. Show how the numbers and operation symbols (addition, subtraction, multiplication, and division) relate to the story and the objects. Make up story questions using your child's name and people she knows in situations and with objects that are familiar to her.

Whenever possible, use real problems. Table setting is an activity that lends itself to meaningful addition or subtraction questions:

Grandma and Grandpa are having dinner with us tonight. How many more chairs should we bring to the table? How many places will we set?

Here are three forks from the dishwasher. How many more do you need to get from the drawer?

When I observe children solving simple problems like these, I am looking for several things besides the right answer. Does the child have a method for finding the answer? Even if the method is more cumbersome than we would like, if it works, that is a sign of developing understanding. It lets us know what to do next. Whether your child needs to arrange the actual objects, can count on fingers, or is able to use mathematical relationships to get the answer, remember to acknowledge the existence of a method that works.

Flexibility is an important part of problem solving in many areas of life, not just mathematics. The method we use to find the answer to an arithmetic question depends on the numbers as well as on the situation. If I have a collection of 100 postcards and give 1 away, I know immediately that I have 99 left. But if my collection contains 3485 postcards and I give 547 of them away, I may want to write down these numbers and use the traditional "borrowing" (now more often referred to as "trading" or "regrouping") method of finding the amount left. The situation is the same, but the numbers are different. We do not want to have our children writing the traditional "borrowing" method in order to solve 100 − 1. If they do, it is a sign to us that they do not understand the relationship of the numbers or that someone has been inappropriately forcing the use of this method. Do more counting forwards and backwards. Line up ten rows of ten objects each, remove one and ask, *How many are left?* Do this with smaller amounts, like 26 or 34, and ask your child how many there are after you take one away, two away, three away. The goal is for her to know the answer without having to count the objects that remain.

With all of these ideas, if it's not enjoyable, your child will not want to participate. If you find your child is resisting, try to see if you are exhibiting impatience or forgot to let her take a turn to make up the questions or games and to be silly. She wants to learn about this vital aspect of the grown-up world. Keep it fun.

Important ideas from chapter 7 for you to think about

▲▽▲▽▲▽▲

Begin with "mental math," asking and answering questions without any writing. Materials for counting should be handy for a child who wants them.

Addition and subtraction questions are closely related. In each, the method of solution depends on which number is missing and also on the size of the numbers.

There are many different ways to find the answer to one question. Help your child move towards increasingly efficient methods as she is ready for them.

We want children to develop flexibility in their methods of solving math problems. Talk about the ways you and your child find answers.

▽▲▽▲▽▲▽

A little bit of counting and a few games played often are best. If you forget to do math for a while, don't overdo it when you remember.

8

Subtraction
A Challenge for Many Children

Although addition and subtraction are tightly intertwined, there are some further considerations about beginning subtraction that deserve their own chapter. Subtraction is much more difficult for children to learn.

The counterpart to "counting on" in addition is "counting back" for subtraction. In order to help children prepare for this, it is necessary for them to learn to count backwards. This is not meaningful before children understand the pattern of the numbers, but many children learn the chant of *ten, nine, eight, seven* . . . before they fully know what it means. Being able to say this is an important start. As the numbers take on meaning, children will be able to use counting backwards as a method of finding a remaining amount.

See chapter 1 for some of the many children's songs that include counting backwards and forwards.

In chapter 7, I listed three different kinds of addition questions. Similarly, there are three different places for an unknown amount in a story that involves "taking" or "giving" away: the unknown number can be the starting quantity, the subtracted amount, or the difference. Let's go back to Cesar and his sister at the school fair.

> *Kelly was at the school fair and won fifteen prize tickets. She saw that her brother had very few and gave him three of hers. How many did she have left?*

> *Kelly was at the school fair and won fifteen prize tickets. The toy she wanted cost only twelve tickets so she gave her extras to her brother. How many did he get from her?*

> *Kelly was at the school fair and won many prize tickets. She saw her little brother and noticed that he only had seven prize tickets, so she gave him three of hers. After that she saw that she had twelve. How many prize tickets did Kelly win?*

Notice that all of these situations involve giving away, which we associate with subtraction, even though the simplest method for solving some of these is addition. How did you do each one?

Another type of question that often involves subtraction is one that deals with comparison. When we ask *How many more...?*, depending on the numbers, we might add or subtract to find the answer. In school, many of us were told that we must always subtract when there is a comparison question.

Notice what you do when you answer the following question:

*Raquel and Jodie are playing a game and have
agreed that the winner will be the first to get 650
points. Jodie has 647 points. How many more does
he need to win?*

Did you add, subtract, or "just know the answer in your
head?" It is much easier to think 647 + 3 = 650 than to
write down the numbers, cross out the "5" and write
"4," and put a little "1" next to the "0" as shown here:

$$6\,\overset{4}{\cancel{5}}{}^{1}0$$
$$-\ 6\ 4\ 7$$
$$\overline{3}$$

THIS IS TOO MUCH WORK!

When the numbers are close together, the difference
should be obvious. Any child who resorts to this
multi-step method to find the answer needs help to
see the relationship of the numbers. It is also possible
that he knows this but needs reassurance that this
easy method is just as legitimate as the longer one that
should be used when the answer is not obvious. Find
out what he is thinking.

Another situation in which the action is subtraction,
but the best method of solution is addition, occurs
when we buy something and get change. It is important to be able to get the answer quickly and "in our
heads." If an item costs 79¢ and we give the cashier
$1.00, it is often quickest to think about groups of
ten: from 79 we need 1 more to reach 80 and then 20
more to reach 100, so the change is 1 + 20 = 21¢. Most
cashiers are trained to give change in an additive way,
saying, for example, *eighty*, as they hand you a penny,
one dollar, as they hand you two dimes, adding up
from the 79¢ to the $1.00. What is the change for an

item costing $6.42 from a ten-dollar bill? 8¢ more than $6.42 brings us to $6.50, 50¢ more brings us to $7.00, and $3.00 more completes the ten, so the answer is $3.58. Did you follow that? If you are not sure, go over it slowly and make up some more questions to practice in your head. In order to help your child, you may have to get more comfortable yourself.

In these last two examples, we are able to find the answer by looking at the difference between two numbers. You may remember that the answer to a subtraction question is called "the difference." When we first teach children about subtraction, it is easiest to teach the meaning of "take away." When we talk about subtraction as "taking away," we begin with a quantity of some object and remove several pieces. This is meaningful to young children and lends itself to the "counting backwards" strategy. But many subtraction questions can be answered by a comparison, and eventually we will need to include this interpretation, too. When we look at the difference between two numbers, we can travel up or down the number line to find the answer.

Number lines are discussed in chapter 1, p.21.

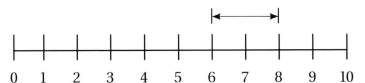

The difference between 6 and 8 is 2. 8 is 2 more than 6. 6 is 2 less than 8.

When creating story questions that might use subtraction, it is helpful to keep in mind that the ideas of "taking away" and separation are unpleasant for many children. Ask questions that separate without a sense of loss, such as these:

Ten students went to the art room. The teacher said they could work with crayons or colored pencils. Four children chose crayons and the rest used the pencils. How many children worked with pencils?

John and his father are decorating party bags for a birthday party with seven children. They finished making three of them. How many more do they need to make?

Our language is so complicated that it is not possible to say that particular words always indicate a specific arithmetic operation. It is necessary to understand the situation described in the question and to choose a method of finding the answer using that knowledge. Ask questions that relate to things you are doing and let your child figure out the solutions. There isn't a fixed way to answer these questions, so listen to your child's method, and if it is not yours, don't assume it's wrong—it could even be a better one!

Important ideas from chapter 8 for you to think about

▲ ▼ ▲ ▼ ▲ ▼ ▲ ▼

There are many different ways to find the answer to a subtraction question, including counting backwards and using addition.

Flexibility remains an important goal. Ask your child questions with easy numbers that encourage the use of a variety of methods. These might include one or two less, ten less, or multiples of ten less.

The phrases "take away" or "give away" are natural ways for young children to understand subtraction, but these terms can also make little ones feel unhappy. Create stories that do not include a sense of loss.

As children get older, they will need to recognize subtraction also as comparison and "difference."

▼ ▲ ▼ ▲ ▼ ▲ ▼ ▲

Your child's way of solving a problem might not be your own. Listen to find out if the method works, then choose the next question.

9

Place Value

Its Role in Addition and Subtraction

The earlier chapters about addition and subtraction (chapters 7 and 8) were limited to small numbers that children can work with in their heads. Eventually, children must be able to add and subtract large quantities quickly, and we need to help them learn ways to do so. It is useful to memorize a procedure, a set of steps that always produces a correct answer.

Such a procedure is called an algorithm. Adults are often in a hurry to have children memorize algorithms. It is important to realize that if you do not build understanding of numbers and of how the algorithms work, your child will not know any more mathematics than if she depended on a calculator.

Our commonly used algorithms rely on clever use of the place value system. As you help your child to see this, you will develop her understanding of the number system as well as her computational skills.

Addition and subtraction algorithms are all too often the beginning of a downward spiral into feeling frustrated and stupid in math, avoiding math whenever possible, and, when it can't be avoided, memorizing without understanding.

Math is too large a subject to be memorized without connections to things you know. Many adults have told me that they got an A in calculus but have no idea what the subject is about. What a waste of time and effort!

As a parent you are also your child's teacher, champion, and friend, and you can help her continue to be a bright and clever mathematician as she learns a "big kid" topic. Comprehension is vital and cannot be overemphasized.

The algorithms for addition and subtraction cause problems primarily when the calculation involves some type of "regrouping."

In the past, the words "carrying" and "borrowing" were used in addition and subtraction. Because both of these require thinking of a quantity as "one ten" and "ten ones" at the same time, the term "regrouping" is now popular.

> We can easily add numbers of any size if we know all the sums of individual digits. For example, to add 387 and 476, many people use this method or "algorithm":
>
> $$\begin{array}{r} {\scriptstyle 1\ 1} \\ 3\ 8\ 7 \\ +\ 4\ 7\ 6 \\ \hline 8\ 6\ 3 \end{array}$$

HOW DO YOU KNOW IF YOUR CHILD IS READY FOR THIS WORK?

1. Your child should understand that two-digit numbers represent tens and ones.

It is necessary to see large numbers as sets of tens and ones, as described in chapter 6. Can your child immediately recognize 5 ten-strips and 3 squares as "53 squares" (or 5 ten-stacks and 3 blocks as "53 blocks")? Is she certain of that number, or does she want to count to make sure? If the latter is the case, do more activities from chapter 6 for understanding the connection between the written two-digit numbers and the quantities they represent. For example, name a number, like "34." Can your child make it without using 34 separate squares? Does she know immediately that with 2 ten-strips she will need 14 loose squares? This will be useful when we do subtraction with regrouping. When we change

$$
\begin{array}{r} 3\,4 \\ -\,1\,8 \\ \hline \end{array}
\quad\text{to}\quad
\begin{array}{r} \overset{2}{\cancel{3}}\,{}^{1}4 \\ -\,1\,8 \\ \hline \end{array}
$$

we are changing the grouping of 34 from 3 tens and 4 ones to 2 tens and 14 ones.

2. Your child understands the concept of addition.

It is important to make a distinction between concept and skill. Before we teach addition of large numbers, it is necessary that your child understand what is meant by addition. At this stage in her life it is sufficient to think of it as joining two groups together. Given an addition question, she may know that she can count out pieces for each group, put the groups together, and find out how many there are in the newly created larger group. Her counting might still be inaccurate. She may have no idea of how to use pencil and paper to make the job easier. In that case your child has the concept, of addition but not the skill with which to carry it out. Before starting to work on any skills with your child, make sure that the concept is understood. This will be true of all the arithmetic processes you want your child to learn.

3. Your child has memorized some basic number facts and is able to add ten to a number immediately.

You can work on addition with place value when your child understands adding as joining two groups together. She should also have begun to memorize some addition facts and be able to use related facts to find answers. For example, *I know that 5 + 5 = 10, so 5 + 6 = 11*. Does your child know 10 more and 10 less than a given number without counting? Can she answer very quickly? Does she see that the new number can be created from the blocks or graph paper by adding or removing a ten-stack as well as by adding or removing 10 ones?

Don't hurry your child into the next level of under-standing if she is not ready. While she may success-fully memorize the steps needed to perform addition and subtraction, you don't want to create a sense that math is not meaningful or not something that she can expect to understand. Trying to learn addition and subtraction with "regrouping" before children are ready is often the beginning of their feeling lost in math. It can be a turning point away from the natural flexibility they have developed in their early math experiences, towards a mistaken idea that there is only one correct way to get the answer.

> You may remember that the answer to a subtraction question is called "the difference."

Adults often forget that answers to subtraction questions like 60 – 59 are much more quickly answered by recognizing the difference between these two numbers than by the tedious steps of regrouping. They sometimes forget to help children maintain the good number sense that lets them immediately see the answer to this question and instead, require that they go through the many-step algorithm to get the answer. If your child can easily find in her head all the sums and differences you pose, move to more difficult questions with larger numbers so that the need for the written algorithm makes sense and is appreciated. This is much better than requiring that she use the rule when she doesn't need it, making math seem like a pointless and boring exercise.

USE "REAL LIFE" QUESTIONS

Look for situations in which you need to add two-digit numbers. When you're waiting in a long line in the grocery store, you and your child can add the cost of some items in your basket. When adding the cost of two items that are each less than $1.00, do you first add the tens and then the ones? Sometimes this method is easier and gives more accurate results. If an item price ends in "9," such as 49¢, how do you add 25¢ to it? Do you turn the 49 into 50, add the 25 to get 75, then subtract 1 to make up for the 1 you added to 49 when you made it 50? Some people take the 1 from the 25 to add on to the 49, changing the question to 50 + 24. All of these methods are good and easier than picturing the written algorithm in your head. As you begin working on two-digit addition with regrouping, make sure you don't discourage these easy tricks when they would naturally be used.

HELPING WITH TWO-DIGIT (OR LARGER) ADDITION

● ● ● ● ● **First we'll look at an addition** of two-digit numbers that does not require regrouping, such as 23 + 45. Have your child use paper and pencil and keep some material handy that can be used to make hundreds, tens, and ones. Remember that it makes no difference whether we add the tens first or the ones first. That rule—to add the ones first—has its place, but it won't be needed right away. As you talk with your child about her work, just listen and do not tell her to change her method. Ask her how she found the answer.

After you ask your child how she found the answer, have her use the base ten materials to show that this is the answer. When a child gets the right answer but is uncertain about it, demonstrating that she is correct builds both understanding and confidence. Even if the correct response was immediate, asking why she thinks this is the right answer is useful. Is she automatically using a column algorithm that she does not understand, or does she see that we can add 2 tens and 4 tens to get 6 tens just as we can add 2 packs of gum and 4 packs of gum to get 6 packs of gum? It is not unusual to have children say, *That was too easy; give me a harder question.* If this happens and the child's work is right, ask her to add two numbers whose sum is greater than 100.

When you see that your child finds these easy, pose questions that can be solved using regrouping ("carrying"). As in the examples given earlier in the chapter about ways we might add in our heads, these can be solved without using the regrouping algorithm. For example, 35 + 28 can be thought of as 35 + 20 + 8 or 35 + 30 -2, as well as other ways. To show your child the regrouping method, you can ask her to use the tens and ones materials to create and then add the numbers. Can she explain how the combinations of ones and tens give the answer? Pay close attention to what she says and do not correct. Remember that even with a question that requires regrouping, the order doesn't matter. When you add 36 and 48 in your head, it is likely that you add the tens first, 30 + 40 = 70, then add the ones, 6 + 8 = 14, and then add 70 + 14 = 84. What matters at this point is that you understand that the "3" in 36 represents 3 tens and that the "4" in 48 represents 4 tens. It is only when we add larger numbers that adding the ones place first becomes a much more efficient way to find the answer. However, it still isn't wrong to add in a different order so long as the meaning of the places is not forgotten:

The usual way to add:	*A way to add that looks odd but is not wrong:*	
	4837	
	+3929	
1 1	7 0 0 0	adding the thousands place
4837	1 7 0 0	adding the hundreds place
+3929	5 0	adding the tens place
	1 6	adding the ones place
8766	8766	adding the separate sums.

This method requires more writing, but it is not wrong.

When children add

$$48$$
$$+\ 35$$

and get an answer of 713, the problem is with their understanding of place value. Scolding them for not doing it correctly and making them practice the traditional method doesn't address the underlying problem, and it will reappear in many other forms. Many children who write "713" for the answer know, when asked, that if we're adding two numbers that are each less than 50, the answer should be less than 100. When they don't understand a rule, they do their best to memorize it, and then stick to their idea because they believe that "the grown-up's rule" must be obeyed.

They think their own ideas and good sense do not matter in this world of rules. Very often children tell me that the wrong answer that's on the paper must be right because this method is the way their teacher or parent says to do it. I have seen children do math correctly in their heads and wrong on paper many, many times. It has become standard procedure for me to ask these questions when I'm asked to evaluate second and third graders. They are so trusting of the grown-ups and also convinced that they have memorized the rule correctly. If children memorize the algorithm correctly, it may be a long time before we find out that they don't know what they are doing. If they memorize it wrong, however, we have the opportunity to help.

So if your child does make mistakes on paper, stay calm. Ask her to do the addition in her head. If she gets a different answer that way, ask her which one she thinks is correct. Have her prove the answer using base ten materials. Then ask which answer she thinks is correct. Show her how the written method relates to what is done with the base ten materials.

If your child adds the tens place first, and adds correctly, see if she seems interested in a way that requires less writing. If so, show her your method and tell why you find it useful. Do not be alarmed if she is not ready to switch to your method. Many children feel attached to their own styles of work. Many are not yet convinced that your method gives the same answer. If the teacher requires the traditional method, your child will soon adopt it. With the work you do at home, there is a much greater chance that she will eventually understand what she is doing, even if the connection is not immediate.

Another way to help your child see why the traditional method is so popular is to ask her to add two numbers in the hundreds, with regrouping in both the tens and ones places. At this point children often find their own system cumbersome and, if they understand what they are doing, readily adopt the traditional style.

If a child is not yet ready to make sense of the traditional algorithm, or wants to keep to her own system, don't argue. It is crucial to avoid getting into a situation in which using your method—and learning the necessary math—becomes losing the fight from the child's point of view. This is a very important principle in all of your dealings with your child.

SUBTRACTING TWO-DIGIT (OR LARGER) NUMBERS

● ● ● ● ● **In chapters 7 and 8** you read about why the meaning of subtraction is more complicated and therefore harder for children to understand than addition. Here I will talk about ideas to keep in mind when you want to help your child learn the mechanics of subtraction with regrouping ("borrowing"). Even though you know a system that you use to carry out subtraction and are capable of telling your child to follow those steps to get an answer, you must help her to understand, as well as to memorize.

Children usually try to do the "right thing," what they think the adults want. A third grade boy told me *minus is easier than plus to me* and that he couldn't understand why his classmates were having a hard time learning subtraction, when he found it so easy. His method of subtracting 178 from 324 was:

AN ERROR IN SUBTRACTION	$3\ ^1 2\ ^1 4$
	$-\ 1\ \ 7\ \ 8$
	$2\ \ 5\ \ 6$

Do you see what he did? He simply turned the 4 ones into 14 and the 2 tens into 12 without regard to the source of those little "1"s. No wonder he found this easier than his classmates! He was so sure of his "good" method that he was not troubled by an incorrect answer. When children think they have memorized a math rule, they stick to it tenaciously, and most do not question whether or not it makes sense.

Ask about your child's thinking!

Remember to ask about your child's thinking no matter whether she got the answer right or wrong. There are two major reasons for this: 1) If you do not know how she got her answer, you have no way of knowing what she is thinking, and so you do not know what to do next. 2) If you only ask children about their thinking when they are wrong, the question, *How did you figure that out?* becomes synonymous with telling them that they are wrong and is no longer a real question.

Many errors are caused by thinking of subtraction as something one does to digits, rather than numbers. Digits are the symbols we use to write the numbers: 0, 1, 2, 3, 4, 5, 6, 7, 8, and 9. These digits are each also a number, so the distinction can be difficult to realize. But when we write the number 203, we are using the digits 0, 2, and 3 to write the number two hundred three. When teachers and parents are in a hurry to have children correctly perform subtraction, they try to teach in a manner that focuses only on the digits and lose sight of the numbers involved. This often causes problems for children.

The following two errors are extremely common. I have seen them repeated countless times. When the digits in the tens and ones places are treated as if they are each individual numbers, one subtraction question is turned into two separate subtraction questions:

AN ERROR IN SUBTRACTION						
$\begin{array}{r}74\\-38\\\hline\end{array}$	became	$\begin{array}{r}7\\-3\\\hline 4\end{array}$	and	$\begin{array}{r}4\\-8\\\hline 4\end{array}$	so	$\begin{array}{r}74\\-38\\\hline 44\end{array}$

This child treated 74 – 38 as the two questions, 4 – 8 and 7 – 3. Then she thought, *I can't take 8 from 4 so they must mean for me to take 4 from 8, which is 4. 7 – 3 is easy, it's 4 so the answer is 44.*

Another student treated 74 – 38 as two separate questions and handled this problem like this:

AN ERROR IN SUBTRACTION						
$\begin{array}{r}74\\-38\\\hline\end{array}$	became	$\begin{array}{r}7\\-3\\\hline 4\end{array}$	and	$\begin{array}{r}4\\-8\\\hline 0\end{array}$	so	$\begin{array}{r}74\\-38\\\hline 40\end{array}$

This child had a similar idea to the one above, but when he saw that he couldn't take 8 from 4, he decided that the result must be 0. Then he subtracted $7 - 3 = 4$ and got an answer of 40.

Another common error is adding instead of subtracting:

$$
\begin{array}{r}
74 \\
- 38 \\
\hline
112
\end{array}
$$

ADDING INSTEAD OF SUBTRACTING

Many students forget to look at the operation symbol "–" and assume that they are supposed to add.

Each of these children was consistent in applying her or his method to several subtraction questions. They listened to the teacher and did what they thought she said to do, doing the closest thing that made sense to them. They tried to bring meaning to something they are not yet ready to handle. The problem is not a lack of attention, but rather a need to understand the place value system.

You may wonder how I knew what the children were thinking. The answer is easy: I asked them. Remember to continue to ask your child about her thinking. In that way, if an error is a careless one, she is likely to find it and correct it herself. It always feels nicer to find your own mistake rather than to have someone else tell you! If a child's ideas are wrong, the next problem becomes yours—what can you do that will cause her to see for herself that the answer is incorrect? Having her act out the problem with base ten materials is a good way.

WHEN IS A CHILD READY TO LEARN A MULTI-DIGIT SUBTRACTION ALGORITHM?

● ● ● ● ● **The first step towards helping** your child is to determine if she understands the concept of subtraction. What does it mean to her when two numbers have that minus sign between them? Does it mean something different when written horizontally, as in $63-17$, from the question written vertically?

$$\begin{array}{r} 63 \\ -\ 17 \\ \hline \end{array}$$

Can your child find the answer to this question in her head? How does she get her answer? If the answer is wrong, is it due to an error in counting backwards, or is there a fundamental error in her method? If the error was in counting backwards, was this a slip in something she knows quite well, or is it a mistake she makes repeatedly?

The answers to these will determine your next steps. If she is shaky about the meaning of subtraction, return to the activities in chapters 6 and 7. If she has a working understanding of subtraction, even if it is limited to "take away," you can use base ten materials to help her develop further understanding about ways to perform subtraction. Ask your child to make the number 45 using as many ten-stacks as possible. Then ask her to give you 18 of those 45 blocks and to find out how many she has left after doing so. In order to do this, she will have to take apart at least one of the ten-stacks. Talk about what happened. Ask, *Why*

did you have to take apart a ten-stack? Write several
subtraction questions, such as:

$$
\begin{array}{ccccc}
35 & 48 & 72 & 84 & 51 \\
-\,23 & -\,26 & -\,35 & -\,41 & -\,18
\end{array}
$$

Ask her if she can predict which ones will require
breaking a ten and which ones won't. If she seems
uncertain, invite her to check her work by using the
materials. If she knows which will require the regrouping, she is ready to learn the subtraction algorithm.

Notice that, as with addition, it does not matter if we
subtract the tens first or the ones. Thus, 53 – 28 can be
treated as two questions:

$$
\begin{array}{ccc}
\begin{array}{r} 53 \\ -\,20 \\ \hline 33 \end{array}
& \text{and then} &
\begin{array}{r} 33 \\ -\,8 \\ \hline 25 \end{array}
\end{array}
$$

Let your child do what makes sense and recognize
that our method was designed to save pencil, paper,
and time. Distinguish between wrong approaches and
inefficient ones.

**Let's use the question $62 - 17$ to talk about algo-
rithms, or methods, of subtraction.** There are several
ways to use the ten that is needed to subtract the
amount in the ones place. A commonly taught system
looks like this:

$$
\begin{array}{ccc}
\begin{array}{r} 62 \\ -\,17 \\ \hline 45 \end{array}
& \text{becomes} &
\begin{array}{r} {}^{5}\!\!\not{6}\,{}^{1}2 \\ -\,1\ 7 \\ \hline 4\ 5 \end{array}
\end{array}
$$

What we do when we use this method is: take 1 of the 6 tens that make 60, add it to the 2 ones. That makes 12 ones from which 7 can be subtracted (12 – 7 = 5) so the difference will have a 5 in the ones place. We then subtract the 10 in 17 from the remaining 5 tens, giving us 4 tens, so the difference is 45.

This method is good because the same pattern works whether we are subtracting two-digit numbers or three-digit or larger. Unlike some of the systems the children use in their heads, it does not get any more cumbersome as we work with larger numbers. It is quick and requires very little writing. Use the base-ten materials to show what you are doing. Paper clips or Lego stacks are good to use because it is evident that "1 ten" is also "10 ones." If this seems uncertain, make sure you spend more time with base ten materials and practicing basic sums.

Some people find it easier, when regrouping is needed, to think of subtracting the amount in the ones place from the 10 instead of from 12. Look at this same example.

$$\begin{array}{r} 62 \\ -\ 17 \end{array} \quad \text{becomes} \quad \begin{array}{r} {}^{5}\cancel{6}\ {}^{10}+2 \\ -\ 1\ \ 7 \end{array}$$

Instead of saying 10 + 2 = 12 and 12 – 7 = 5, we are saying 10 – 7 = 3 and 3 + 2 = 5. We subtract 7 from the 10 taken from the tens place, leaving 3; these 3 plus the 2 that were in the ones place of 62 together make 5 ones in the answer. Next, we subtract the 1 ten of 17 from the remaining 5 tens of 62, giving a difference of 45.

This method has a tremendous advantage. Once you

know the pairs of sums that make ten (9 + 1, 8 + 2, 7 + 3, 6 + 4, and 5 + 5), no more subtraction facts need to be known! This algorithm, too, works no matter how large the numbers are. If you had trouble understanding how this method works, you may be in a similar position to that of your child trying to learn subtraction. Feel free to take some base ten materials and work on this yourself. You can work with your child to see if you can make sense of it together.

As you work with your child, remember that your task is threefold. Most important, you are trying to help your child learn algorithms for multi-digit addition and subtraction, but do not lose sight of the fact that you are also trying to help build your child's mathematical confidence and belief in herself as a problem solver. The third important job is to keep your mathematical relationship with your child a friendly one, so that it can continue through many years.

Important ideas from chapter 9 for you to think about

△▽△▽△▽△▽△

Errors in multi-digit addition and subtraction are usually caused by inadequate understanding of the place values in our number system. Work to build your child's understanding of place value.

Encourage your child to stay flexible and to use a variety of ways to compute. Do not use algorithms to replace good methods of calculating in your head. Each method has its place. Figuring 60 – 59 should not require all the steps of the algorithm.

▽△▽△▽△▽△▽

Don't hurry your child. Rushing to learn the arithmetic algorithms without understanding place value is the beginning of most children's difficulty with math.

10

Patterns

Algebra

Mathematics can be defined as the study of patterns. While we think of numbers as the basis of mathematics, the ability to find patterns plays a central role. Children take comfort in patterns. They like a day to have order. Ask a kindergarten teacher what happens when the schedule is changed. She is certain to get a complaint from the children: *But we do math **after** recess, not before!* That is probably why children are so fond of counting—they like things to be orderly and predictable, and the order of the numbers is always the same. As noted in chapter 1, children who are learning to count must be able to use the repetition of the one-through-nine pattern in order to count above twenty.

There are two basic types of patterns: those that repeat and those that grow.

Arithmetic, algebra, and geometry may seem to have little in common, but they are closely related. You may remember, from high school, using algebra to write equations of lines. This was part of "coordinate geometry." Algebra also lets us generalize arithmetic properties, relationships, and patterns, like the fact that when we add two even numbers, the sum is always even. Arithmetic algorithms and math formulas are also the result of people's pattern detection.

1. Repeating patterns—a wallpaper design, bricks in a wall, a picket fence:

A word for the smallest repeated part of a repeating pattern is its "core." For example, the core of the pattern **ABABABAB** is **AB**. The core of **ABBAABBAABBA** is **ABBA**, a tricky one for children to see. Count how many pieces are in the core. With your child, you can figure out how many pieces will be in two, three, or more repetitions—which is preparation for learning multiplication.

2. Growing patterns (notice that these do not have a core):

Numbers: Our numbers form a growing pattern.

0	1	2	3	4	5	6	7	8	9
10	11	12	13	14	15	16	17	18	19
20	21	22	23	24	25	26	27	28	29 ...

Boxes or Legos can be used to make the growing pattern 1, 3, 6, 10, 15 ... You can see why these are called "triangular numbers."

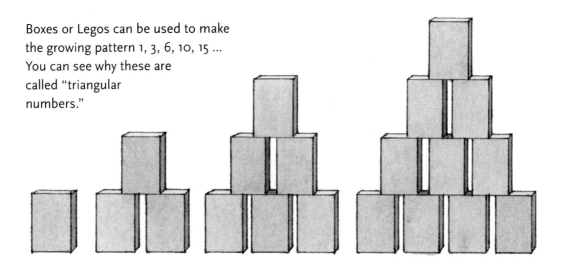

Cans placed in pyramids form the "pyramidal numbers." The first three are 1, 4, 10. Do you see how they relate to the triangular numbers? (Each level is a triangular number.)

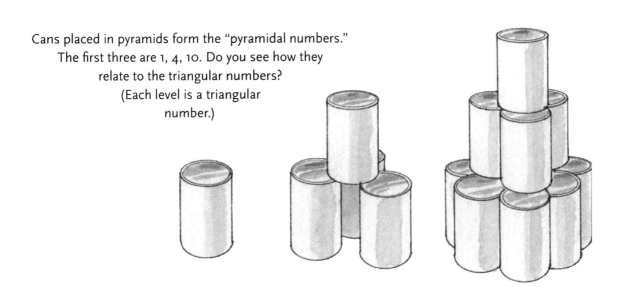

If you did not read chapter 3 in which there is a discussion of attribute recognition, you may want to do so before continuing.

Be aware of the difference between these two types of patterns and talk about which kind of pattern you see or make.

Children enjoy spotting patterns and predicting what comes next. You can take turns making a pattern and having the other person continue. You can begin with simple **ABAB** patterns using different colors, shapes, sizes, textures, sounds, motions, and other attributes.

After a few rounds, make sure to progress to patterns other than **ABAB**. You can limit the number of attributes by using materials that are exactly alike, such as toothpicks, paper clips, a set of spoons, and forming a pattern by their placement. You can also find materials that are the same except for one trait, like some Legos or plastic, screw-top bottle caps, which are the same except for color.

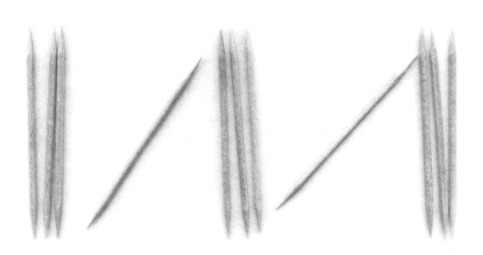

The toothpicks used to make this pattern all look the same.
The position in which they were placed forms the pattern.

The only difference in these forks is size, and that one attribute (size) forms the pattern.

Here, two different characteristics are used to form the pattern:
type of utensil (fork or spoon) and the size (large or small).

Now, position has been added as a third variable.
With very few materials, complex patterns can be made.

Of course, food is an excellent material for creating patterns. The varieties of colors and shapes lend themselves to imaginative design. Carrots, celery, cucumbers, and green beans can all be used as sticks. Circular cucumber slices, curls of green pepper, and peas provide curves. Crackers can be rectangular, round, or many other interesting shapes. Raisins and peanuts also make fine design elements. Wash hands and have fun.

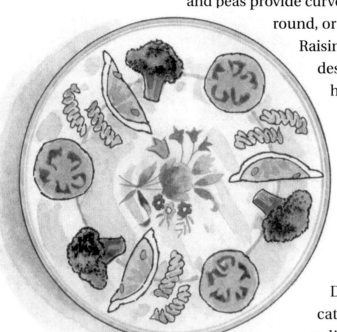

Food provides endless possibilities for having fun with patterns.

Look for patterns outdoors, too. Buildings often have patterns of windows or bricks. In a housing development, the buildings themselves may form a pattern. Telephone wires and poles make another. Decorative tiles can have intricate patterns. Remember that you are discussing this with a youngster, so do not be too exacting in your requirements: accept a close-enough match to form a pattern. Don't be surprised if your child uses this as an opportunity to be strict with you, taking advantage of a rare opportunity to correct you. This is normal. Explain your thinking and move on.

Riding in the car, the non-drivers can take turns initiating "snap, clap" patterns with their fingers. Everyone can participate in verbal pattern games. The child who is learning to read will benefit from patterns made by words that start with the same sounds, such as "mad, milk, mud, mom, more . . ." or, more challenging, "mommy, daddy, monkey, dog, muffin, donut . . ." It is fun to take turns and see how many words you can find.

When you engage in these activities, you are actually paving the way for your child's understanding of algebra. Formulas written with letters in algebra class are just a way to describe a pattern. Although algebra will not be taught formally until middle school, the gradual increase in your child's ability to recognize and describe patterns will help create a solid foundation for this important subject.

Example of a pattern that is an algebra formula:

If one can of cat food costs $1.05, then two cans cost 2 x $1.05 or $2.10, and three cans cost 3 x $1.05 or $3.15. We can generalize this to say if "N" is the number of cans I buy, then the total cost is (N x $1.05). We can go even further to notice that for any fixed-price item we buy, the Number we buy times the Price of each one is the total Cost. In algebra this can be written as N x P = C.

Important ideas from chapter 10 for you to think about

▲▽▲▽▲▽▲▽▲▽

Children naturally look for patterns to help them make sense of the world.

Patterns exist all around us and can be used to develop mathematical thinking, language, and artistic sense.

Encourage your child to find and describe patterns of all kinds.

▽▲▽▲▽▲▽▲▽▲

Playing with patterns—in blocks, food, clapping rhythms—provides another relaxing way for you to engage in math with your child. This is a natural place for your child to take the lead.

In Conclusion

I hope that now you feel ready to help your children learn math and have confidence in their ability to learn and do well. You can provide the best support for your children's future as you develop their ability to learn and understand the world. In school, your children are likely to be one of 25 students in a class. This means that they can receive very little individual time from the teacher. As you listen carefully to your children's words, you are the person most likely to notice things they do not understand. You may experience moments of disappointment, but move on and plan activities to make those things clear. You will also know exactly which facts they need to memorize next, and to focus on just one fact until it is known thoroughly. This is true if they skip 14 when counting, or know most of the sums to 10 but forget 4 + 6. In Volume 2, I'll provide activities for learning the multiplication tables and continuing work in all branches of math. In the meantime, play with numbers and talk about math!

Other Resources

Books for you to enjoy with your children or that suggest activities for you to do together

The public library has many fine counting books in the Picture Book section. Borrow any interesting titles and buy some that you and your children especially enjoy. Some of my favorite books are listed here. These are older titles that might not be in your local bookstore.

Mitsumasa Anno

Anno's books are as wonderful for the art as for the mathematics. Find copies at the library or out-of-print booksellers and treasure them. *Math Games* contains many math topics including a simpler, five-piece tangram puzzle that can be cut from and reassembled into a square.

> *Anno's Math Games*
> NY: Philomel Books, 1997.
> *Anno's Counting House*
> NY: Philomel Books, 1982.

Maja Apelman and Julie King

Exploring Everyday Math: Ideas for Students,
Teachers, & Parents
   Portsmouth, NH: Heinemann, 1993.

Mary Baratta-Lorton
This is another out-of-print book that is well worth finding. It is full of activities that prepare children for both reading and math. The game "Break the Stack Behind Your Back" and the version with pennies under a cup described in chapter 7 were inspired by "Hide 'n' Go Seek" on pages 114–115 of this excellent book.

Workjobs . . . For Parents: Activity-Centered Learning
in the Home
   Menlo Park, CA: Addison-Wesley, 1975.

Tana Hoban
Tana Hoban has written very many books that help develop young children's spatial and visual awareness. Look for others, too.

Shapes, Shapes, Shapes
   NY: Greenwillow Books/HarperCollins, 1996.

Peggy Kaye

Games for Learning: Ten Minutes a Day to Help Your Child
Do Well in School—From Kindergarten to Third Grade
   NY: Farrar, Straus and Giroux, 1991.

Jan Mokros

Beyond Facts & Flashcards: Exploring Math with Your Kids
   Portsmouth, NH: Heinemann, 1996.

Peggy Parish

> *Amelia Bedelia*
> NY: HarperCollins 1992.

Jean Kerr Stenmark and Grace Davila Coates
> *Family Math for Young Children: Comparing*
> CA: Equals, 1997.

Ann Tompert and Robert Andrew Parker
> *Grandfather Tang's Story* (a tangram book)
> Dragonfly Books, 1997.

Books that will educate you further about children's math thinking and learning

Herbert P. Ginsberg
Herbert Ginsberg's books demonstrate careful observation and deep thoughtfulness, while being a delight to read.

> *Children's Arithmetic*: *How They Learn It and How You Teach It*
> Austin, TX: Pro-Ed, 1989.

Herbert P. Ginsberg, et al.
> *Big Math For Little Kids* (series)
> Upper Saddle River,NJ: Pearson Prentice Hall, 2003.

Constance Kamii and Leslie Baker Housman
> *Young Children Reinvent Arithmetic: Implication of Piaget's Theory*
> NY: Teachers College Press, 1999.

Kathy Richardson

Kathy Richardson has written many books and made videos about children's math thinking and easy ways to assess it.

Developing Number Concepts, Book 1: Counting, Comparing, and Pattern
Dale Seymour Publications, 1998.
Developing Number Concepts, Book 2: Addition and Subtraction
Dale Seymour Publications, 1998.

Kathy Richardson, Lucinda O'Neill, and Linda Starr

Developing Math Concepts in Pre-Kindergarten
Bellingham, WA: Math
Perspectives, 2008.

Catherine Stern

The Structural Arithmetic series of workbooks for children using Stern Blocks (some also by Margaret Stern) are another excellent way to develop children's understanding of numbers. (These authors are no relation to me.)

Children Discover Arithmetic: An Introduction to Structural Arithmetic
NY: HarperCollins, 1971.

Acknowledgments

So many people have contributed to the work and thoughts that went into this book that it is not possible to list them all. I will limit this list to the most influential, with my deep appreciation and apologies to anyone I have omitted.

My thanks to the teachers and principals at Central Park East I (1988–2000) who welcomed me into their classrooms, especially Susan Gordon who taught me much about teaching, enthusiastically learned more math and math pedagogy, and shared her enthusiasm with her students and her students with me. To Donnie Rotkin who taught his unsure students to touch their heads as a reminder that they can hold a number there. To the parents who requested workshops to help them help their children and for whom I wrote a monthly math column. And especially to Tova, who allowed me to volunteer to teach math in her classroom, even though it was embarrassing to have her mom revealed as "Nerd of the World!" and for her patient help with the title, support, and editing.

The categorization of types of addition and subtraction questions I learned from the publications of the Cognitively Guided Instruction group at the University of Wisconsin, Madison.

My great appreciation to those friends who, as experts in their fields, generously contributed their skills. Each one of them was enthusiastic about the importance of my work and contributed to my perseverance. Francesca Bacon, who volunteered to help me with the video and website, and then stayed to give me advice on the visual aspects of the book, promotional ideas, and staunch support. Kallyn Krash, who generously edited the text, with patience and clarity, a labor that cannot be sufficiently thanked. Ben Sadok, wise copy editor. Rachel Perkins, artistic cover designer. Adrian and Elizabeth Kitzinger designers, compositors, attentive readers and more, who completely understood the importance of making the book clear and appealing.

My daughter Clara, who enthusiastically encouraged my work and realized that the best way to illustrate the book is with video. Sandra Matthews, photographer, whose archives contained the photo of me with my daughters. Jonathan Bell of BellPro, who videotaped the children and the parent workshop with complete understanding of the purpose and took on the role of director when he saw that it was needed. David Elgart, who patiently taught me to use Geometer's Sketchpad for the diagrams.

And my great thanks to my husband, Ben, whose support made the entire project possible.

Sample Materials
to Use at Home

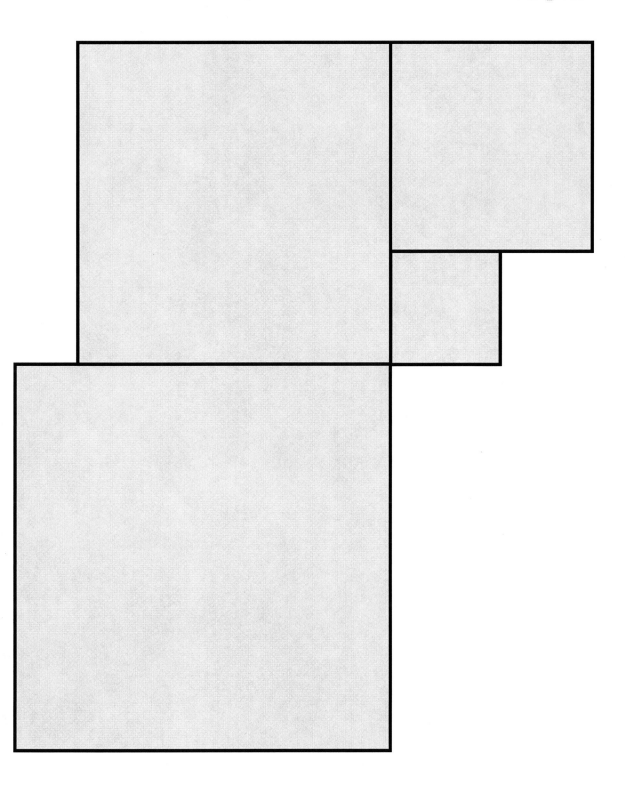

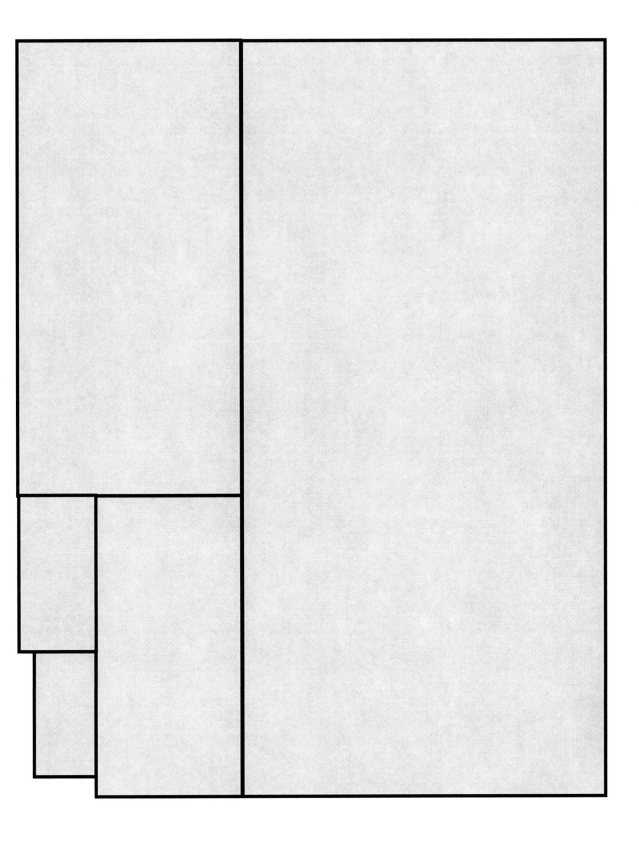

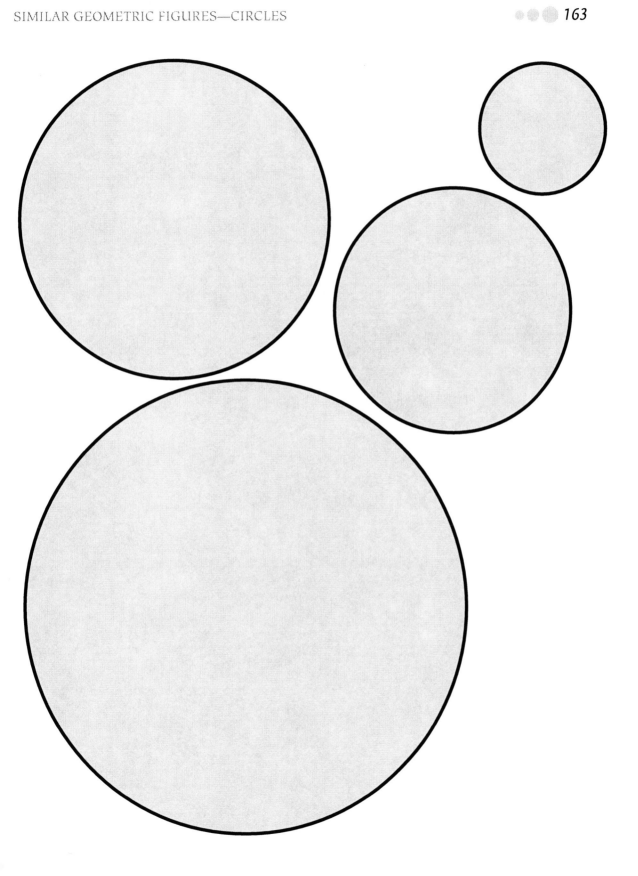

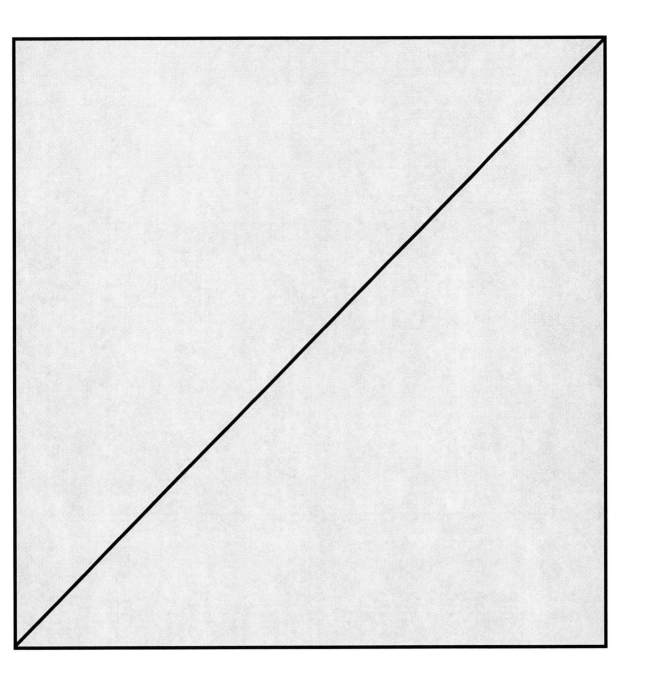

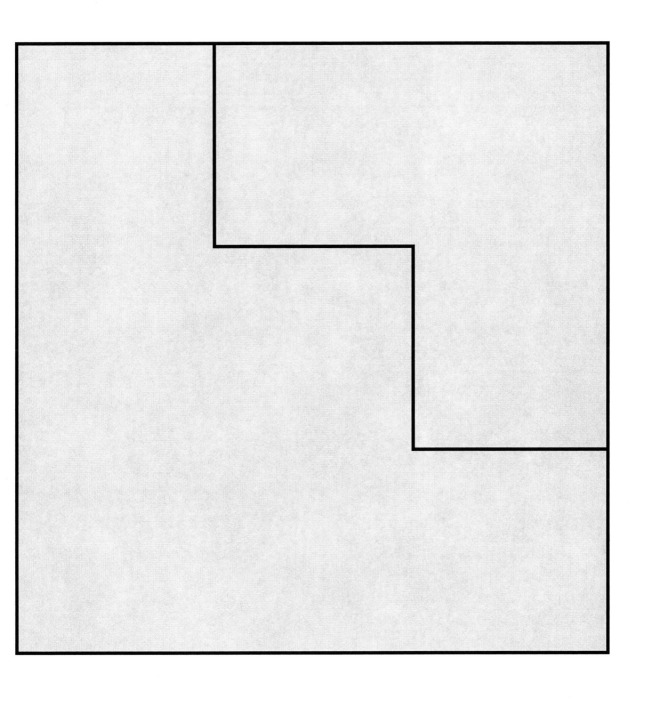

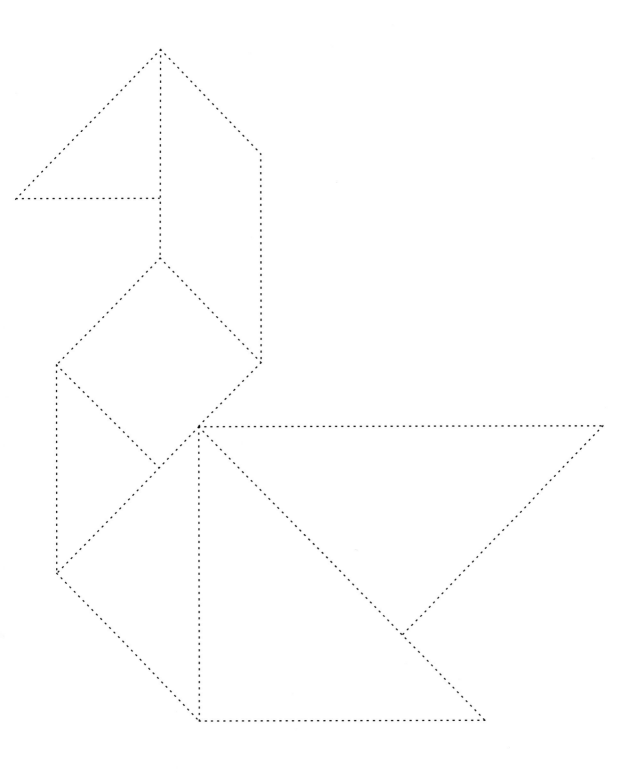

ABOUT THE AUTHOR

Frances Stern has taught math for nearly 50 years—not because she is so ancient, but because as a child, teachers and neighbors recruited her assistance. She holds a master's degree in mathematics and worked in the computer industry. When her children started school, she saw that math was often taught in a manner that left many students bored or lost. She volunteered in the classroom, and soon parents requested that she hold evening sessions to prepare them to help their children. Her enjoyment of these activities led her to change careers. She has since taught math at all levels from pre-school through college, specializing in teacher training. Her many workshops have been appreciatively and enthusiastically received by parents, teachers, caregivers, and families at branches of the New York Public Library; PTAs at New York City public and private schools; NYC teachers, Regional Math Coordinators, and District Vice Principals; parent coordinators of New Vision Schools; and professional organizations. Her articles have been published by the National Council of Teachers of Mathematics and New Visions for Public Schools. "My secret agenda is to use math as a way to improve the relationship between children and adults: when children share their ideas about math, adults are often impressed, and it changes the quality and nature of their discussions."

FORTHCOMING

Volume 2: For Parents of Children in Grades 3–6

It's Time for the Times Tables — Beginning Multiplication
Heading for the Big Times — Multiplication of Large Numbers
Getting a Fair Share — Beginning Division
Measuring Up — Fractions and Decimals through Measurement
Taking Things Apart — Fractions
Taking Things Apart — Decimals
Divvying Up — More about Division
Understanding the World — Statistics
Getting in Shape — Geometry
There's a Pattern to It — Algebra
Tricks of the Trade — Problem-Solving Techniques
Is It Fair? — Probability

Games & Gifts
Other Resources
Sample Materials

Breinigsville, PA USA
17 January 2011
253464BV00004B/41-84/P